LEGENDARY
SIRES

SHOWJUMPERS EDITION

Volume I

Mathilde Chereau
and
Michael Beas

Legendary Sires: Showjumpers Edition Volume I
By Mathilde Chereau and Michael Beas
Published by Atlas Elite Publishing

Atlas Elite Publishing

www.atlaselitepublishingpartners.com

This book is a work of nonfiction. Every effort has been made to ensure the accuracy of the information presented. However, the publisher and authors disclaim any liability for errors or omissions.

Images, data, and references cited in this book have been used with permission or fall under fair use guidelines.

ISBN: 978-1-962825-36-8
First Edition: 2025

For permissions or inquiries, contact Atlas Elite Publishing

ATLAS ELITE
PARTNERS
PUBLISHING

TABLE OF CONTENTS

Part II: The Foundation Stallions in Modern Breeding 1970's - 1990's

Part III: The Stallions and Their Riders
- Legends in Show Jumping

INTRODUCTION

This inaugural volume offers a fascinating journey into the legacy of foundational stallions that have shaped the modern world of showjumping. It seeks to provide readers with an in-depth understanding of how these extraordinary horses continue to influence both breeding and sport. While it is impossible to capture the entirety of the showjumping breeding landscape, we have chosen to highlight some of the most iconic and impactful stallions whose influence is undeniable.

For generations, breeders have meticulously worked to refine and enhance the genetic potential of their horses, driven by the ambition to produce superior showjumpers. As the sport and industry of showjumping have evolved, so too have the demands placed on stallions and their progeny. The stallions featured in this volume represent the very foundation of contemporary showjumping, embodying the traits and qualities that define excellence in the sport today.

Traditionally, the art of equine breeding has centered on the strategic pairing of sire and dam to maximize the genetic potential of their offspring. While the science of genetics undoubtedly plays a vital role, experienced horsemen know that breeding alone is only one part of the equation. The success of a performance horse depends not only on its inherited traits but also on the nurturing care, training, and opportunities provided throughout its life.

To delve deeper into this intricate interplay between nature and nurture, we have chosen to focus on the development of these stallions through the perspectives of those most intimately involved in their journey: the riders, trainers, and breeders. Through their insights, we explore the unique connections between horse and rider, as well as the vital collaboration between rider and breeder that contributes to the development of a champion.

Before we embark on this exploration, it is important to acknowledge the foundational role of certain Thoroughbred stallions whose bloodlines are woven into the pedigrees of today's showjumping elite. These trailblazing stallions represent a starting point for modern breeding and include:

- **Ibrahim**
- **Almé**
- **Furioso**
- **Ladykiller**
- **Rantzau**

By examining the influence of these Thoroughbreds and the enduring legacy of their descendants, this volume offers a deeper appreciation of the careful artistry and science that underpin the world of showjumping breeding. Welcome to a celebration of these equine legends and the extraordinary impact they have had—and continue to have—on the sport we cherish.

CHAPTER 1

IBRAHIM
1952

			ORANGE PEEL XX	JUS D'ORANGE XX
			xx 046606419	xx 1912
		THE LAST ORANGE	1919 Brown	
		SF 25000159021852M	Lic.: xx	RIRETTE XX
		1941 Brown		xx 1913
		Lic.: SF		
			VELLEDA	HORLOGER
			SF 25000149516376B	SF 1907
			1921 Brown	
IBRAHIM				LAPIN (N.C.)
Stallion 1952 Brown 1.66 m				SF 1911
SF 25000159000207P				
Lic.: SF			PORTE BONHEUR	ROYAL CHESNUT
			SF 25000158500509P	SF 1917
			1937 Chestnut	
	VAILLANTE		Lic.: SF	HISTOIRE
	SF 25000149002055W			SF 1929
	1943 Chestnut			
			QUERQUEVILLE	VAS-Y-DONC
			SF 25000149501390Q	SF 1921
			1938 Chestnut	
				CANCALE
				SF 1925

🐾 39.26% 🐴 INBREEDING COEFFICIENT

In the annals of showjumping history, few names resonate as profoundly as Ibrahim. Born in 1952, this remarkable stallion emerged from modest beginnings to leave an indelible mark on the sport, shaping the genetic foundation of countless champions. His story is one of perseverance, evolving perceptions, and ultimate triumph—a testament to the transformative power of exceptional breeding.

Origins and Early Promise

Ibrahim's lineage is rooted in strength and resilience. His sire, The Last Orange xx, brought Thoroughbred refinement, while his dam, Vaillante, contributed robust Normandy bloodlines. Vaillante proved to be a prolific producer, delivering several notable studs when paired with the stallion Gagne Si Peu. Among her offspring, Ibrahim stood out early, catching the discerning eye of Alfred Lefevre. Recognizing his potential, Lefevre purchased the young stallion, and Ibrahim did not disappoint. As a youngster, he dominated the in-hand show circuit, winning accolades for his striking conformation and undeniable presence.

Physically, Ibrahim was a marvel. His long neck and withers gave him elegance and reach, while his supple back and well-angled shoulders ensured flexibility and power. His strong upper legs, combined with low-set knees and hocks, provided the perfect blend of strength and agility—traits essential for the rigors of showjumping. Despite these attributes, his journey to recognition was far from straightforward.

Early Challenges and Misjudgment

Initially, the Normandy breeders were skeptical of Ibrahim's quality. In their eyes, he seemed suited only for cob mares—a pairing considered beneath the aspirations of elite breeding at the time. This misconception limited his opportunities in the early years and relegated him to a modest role. Ultimately, he was sold to the Saint-Lô French National Stud, where he became a public stallion. It was a turning point that would set the stage for his eventual rise to prominence.

A Turning Point in the 1970s

Ibrahim's true potential began to unfold in the 1970s when his progeny started dominating showjumping finals. His offspring exhibited the same physical traits and competitive spirit that defined him, proving his worth as a sire of champions. Remarkably, while Ibrahim produced more daughters than sons, it was his male progeny that propelled his legacy to new heights. Chief among them was the legendary Almé, a stallion who would carry Ibrahim's influence far beyond his lifetime.

The Enduring Impact of Ibrahim's Lineage

The measure of Ibrahim's greatness lies not only in the achievements of his immediate offspring but also in the enduring success of his bloodline. At the 2014 World Equestrian Games (WEG), a staggering 36 horses traced their lineage back to Ibrahim. Nearly fifty years after his prime, his genetic influence remained a dominant force in the sport—an extraordinary feat that underscores his unparalleled contribution to showjumping.

Ibrahim's story is a reminder of the importance of perseverance and vision in the world of equine breeding. Though initially underestimated, his remarkable qualities ultimately earned him the recognition he deserved. Today, his legacy lives on in the countless champions who carry his blood, proving that greatness, though sometimes slow to be acknowledged, is impossible to ignore.

In the chapters ahead, we will explore the lives and achievements of other foundational stallions, but few can rival the profound and lasting impact of Ibrahim. His story is a cornerstone of modern showjumping—a legacy that continues to inspire breeders, riders, and enthusiasts around the globe.

CHAPTER 2

ALMÉ

1966

ALME 🔵✅
Stallion 1966 Brown 1.66 m
SF 25000160001122N
Lic.: AWR, BWP, HANN, KWPN, SF
1.60m Jump.

IBRAHIM 🔵✅
SF 25000159000207P
1952 Brown 1.66 m
Lic.: SF

THE LAST ORANGE 🔵✅
SF 25000159021852M
1941 Brown
Lic.: SF

ORANGE PEEL XX 🔵✅
xx 1919

VELLEDA 🔵✅
SF 1921

VAILLANTE 🔵✅
SF 25000149002055W
1943 Chestnut

PORTE BONHEUR 🔵✅
SF 1937

QUERQUEVILLE 🔵✅
SF 1938

GIRONDINE 🔵✅
SF 25000150066351C
1950 Brown 1.67 m

ULTIMATE XX 🔵✅
xx
1941 Bay 1.66 m
Lic.: SF

UMIDWAR XX 🔵✅
xx 1931

NO GO XX 🔵✅
xx 1934

J'VINS MARS 🔵✅
SF 25000149018541B
1931 Bay 1.60 m

CYRUS 🔵✅
SF 1924

MAZETTE 🔵✅
SF 1925

💧 62.11% 🐎 INBREEDING COEFFICIENT

Few stallions have had as profound an impact on showjumping as **Almé**, a direct descendant of Ibrahim and the exceptional dam line of Girondine. Girondine herself was a remarkable producer, having delivered three licensed and successful jumpers in addition to Almé. Often heralded as **"the father of 20th-century breeding,"** Almé's legacy transcends his immediate accomplishments, shaping the modern showjumping landscape in an extraordinary way.

Early Success and Progeny

During his first four years in France, Almé solidified his reputation as a sire of champions. Among his early offspring were international showjumping legends Galoubet A, I Love You, and Jalisco B. Each of these stallions left an indelible mark on the sport:

- **Galoubet A**: The father of Quick Star and the three-time World Cup winner Baloubet du Rouet.
- **I Love You**: A two-time World Cup winner who dominated international arenas.
- **Jalisco B**: The sire of superstar stallion Quidam de Revel, a foundational figure in modern breeding.

Almé's influence extended well beyond France. While standing at Zangersheide, his progeny were registered in the Hanoverian stud book, where they had a transformative effect. His bloodlines also entered the prestigious Holstein stud books through his sons Ahorn Z, Aloubé Z, Athlet Z, and Alexis Z. Notably, his grandson, Quidam de Revel, continued this legacy by further contributing to Holstein breeding.

Challenges and Resilience

Despite his remarkable achievements, Almé was not without faults. A predisposition to scrotal hernias emerged in his progeny, leading to several sons and grandsons undergoing operations and, in some cases, losing a testicle. Almé himself underwent surgery in 1984, becoming a monorchid. Yet this challenge did little to diminish his enduring influence on breeding and sport.

The Father of World Breeding

In the 2003 edition of *Annuaire Monneron*, Bernard le Courtois eloquently described Almé as the "father of world breeding," underscoring his unparalleled contributions to the sport. Le Courtois noted Almé's increasing importance across major breeding countries, citing the 2002 World Championships in Jerez as a prime example. In the final—where riders swapped horses— three of the four contenders (one stallion and three mares) descended from Almé, comprising an astonishing 75% of the field.

Le Courtois also highlighted the enduring value of Almé's lineage, particularly through mares carrying his bloodline. As an example, the best six-year-old in Europe that year, Mozart des Hayettes, featured Almé twice in his pedigree. This exemplifies the wisdom of investing in mares from Almé's dynasty to produce horses of exceptional quality.

Global Demand and Enduring Influence

Almé's influence was not confined to Europe. His reputation crossed the Atlantic, with American breeders willing to pay significant sums to incorporate his bloodlines. This enthusiasm was bolstered by the success of his son, Galoubet A, who had been purchased by a syndicate in the United States a year earlier. Almé's impact on breeding programs worldwide cemented his status as a valuable and sought-after asset in the pedigrees of sport horses.

Conclusion

Almé's legacy is one of unparalleled influence and excellence. From his extraordinary progeny to his far-reaching genetic impact, he stands as a cornerstone of modern showjumping. As the "father of 20th-century breeding," Almé's story continues to inspire breeders and riders, reminding us of the enduring power of exceptional bloodlines in shaping the future of the sport.

CHAPTER 3

FURIOSO II
1939

			PRECIPITATION XX	HURRY ON XX
			xx 276306064014933	xx 1913
			1933 Chestnut	
		FURIOSO XX	Lic.: xx	DOUBLE LIFE XX
		xx		xx 1926
		1939 Bay 1.66 m		
		Lic.: SF		SON-IN-LAW XX
			MAUREEN XX	xx 1911
			xx	
FURIOSO II			1931 Dark brown	ST. PRISCA XX
Stallion 1965 Chestnut 1.67 m				xx 1926
SF 25000159040975B				
Lic.: BADWU, BAVAR, HANN, HESS, OLDBG, RHEI			TALISMAN	LE ROYAL
			SF 25000159000767F	SF 1933
			1941 Chestnut	
		DAME DE RANVILLE	Lic.: SF	KREOLE
		SF 2500014900368E		SF 1932
		1947 Chestnut		
			QUE JE SUIS BELLE	LORD ORANGE
			SF 25000149500289M	SF 1933
			1938 Chestnut	
				KOMEDIE
				SF 1932

🜄 59.96% 🐎 INBREEDING COEFFICIENT

Furioso II's journey from France to Germany marked the beginning of a transformative era for European sport horse breeding. Imported in 1968 by the visionary breeder George Vorwerk, Furioso II became a cornerstone of the Oldenburg breed. His unique blend of Thoroughbred refinement and sport horse versatility reshaped the breeding landscape, earning him the nickname "Stamp Stallion" for his ability to pass on his exceptional traits.

A Stellar Pedigree

Furioso II was born into an impressive lineage. His dam, Dame de Renville, was a prolific producer, giving rise to several notable horses, including Mexico, Laeken, Jexico de Parc, and Heur de Bratand. This maternal line, combined with the Thoroughbred influence of his sire, endowed Furioso II with the genetic foundation to excel as a breeding stallion.

A New Era for Oldenburg Breeding

In 1967, Furioso II was approved for the Oldenburg studbook, a pivotal moment for the breed. George Vorwerk's decision to import Furioso II introduced a modern type of sport horse to Oldenburg lines without resorting to pure Thoroughbreds. This strategic integration of Thoroughbred blood elevated the breed, enhancing its athleticism and elegance while maintaining its strength and reliability.

Furioso II's physical attributes were nothing short of remarkable. His offspring inherited his "very good feet and legs," ensuring soundness and durability. His "outstanding neck and shoulder" conferred balance and power, key traits for success in sport. Additionally, his striking dappled chocolate chestnut coat with a flaxen tail and distinctive white markings made him a visually iconic figure in the breeding world.

Expanding Influence

Furioso II's impact extended far beyond Oldenburg breeding. He was later approved for the Hanoverian, Rhineland, and Westphalian studbooks, further solidifying his reputation as a transformative sire. His genetic influence permeated these breeding programs, shaping modern sport horses with his hallmark traits of athleticism, soundness, and refinement.

The "Stamp Stallion"

The nickname "Stamp Stallion" was well-earned, as Furioso II consistently passed on his defining characteristics to his progeny. Breeders praised his ability to imprint his offspring with his excellent conformation, making him a reliable choice for improving the quality of future generations. His legacy lives on through the countless champions who trace their lineage back to him.

Conclusion

Furioso II's importation to Germany was a watershed moment for European breeding. His profound influence on the Oldenburg, Hanoverian, Rhineland, and Westphalian breeds revolutionized the modern sport horse. As a "Stamp Stallion," Furioso II not only shaped the physical and athletic qualities of his descendants but also set a new standard for excellence in equine breeding. His story remains an enduring testament to the power of vision and innovation in the world of sport horses.

CHAPTER 4

LADYKILLER XX

1961

LADYKILLER XX 🔵✅
Stallion 1961 Brown 1.64 m
xx 276306064000861
Lic.: HOLST, xx

SAILING LIGHT XX 🔵✅
xx 276306064006849
1949 Chestnut
Lic.: xx

BLUE PETER XX 🔵✅
xx 276306064181636
1936 Chestnut
Lic.: xx

FAIRWAY XX 🔵✅
xx 1925

FANCY FREE XX 🔵✅
xx 1924

SOLAR CYGNET XX 🔵✅
xx
1940 Brown

HYPERION XX 🔵✅
xx 1930

SWEET SWAN XX 🔵✅
xx 1927

LONE BEECH XX 🔵✅
xx 276306064953839
1939 Brown

LOANINGDALE XX 🔵✅
xx
1929 Brown
Lic.: xx

COLORADO XX 🔵✅
xx 1923

PERFECTION XX 🔵✅
xx 1918

FARTUCH XX 🔵✅
xx
1932 Brown

APRON XX 🔵✅
xx 1920

BOIARINIA XX 🔵✅
xx 1926

💧 100.00% 🐴 INBREEDING COEFFICIENT

Ladykiller stands as the most influential Thoroughbred stallion in the history of German sport horse and show jumping breeding. As the founder of the Holsteiner L-line, his legacy is unparalleled. With 36 licensed stallion offspring, many of whom have become icons in their own right—such as the legendary Landgraf I and Lord—Ladykiller's contributions have left an indelible mark on equestrian history.

A Thoroughbred with Exceptional Qualities

Dr. Dietrich Rossow, in his *Stallion Book of the Holsteiner Warmblood Breed*, provides a detailed and insightful assessment of Ladykiller:

> "He was an average-sized, clearly masculine type with a beautiful head, a really heavy neck, good shoulder, rather flat loin, and a nicely coupled, heavily muscled croup. He had first-rate legs and feet for a Thoroughbred and was an elastic mover. He was everything a state breeding program could wish for. With his 35 approved sons and 195 approved daughters, he has had the greatest impact of all on the Holsteiner breed."

Ladykiller's conformation and athleticism were ideal for breeding performance horses. His "first-rate legs and feet," combined with his "elastic" movement, made him a valuable asset to Holsteiner breeding programs, particularly for producing sport horses capable of excelling in show jumping.

Strategic Crosses and Superior Offspring

Ladykiller's ability to elevate the Holsteiner breed came through his strategic pairing with mares that carried some Thoroughbred blood. This was critical in producing his best offspring—horses that embodied a balance of power, elegance, and athleticism.

Interestingly, Dr. Rossow noted that Ladykiller's influence varied depending on the mares he was paired with:

> "When crossed with coarse, common mares, Ladykiller produced accordingly. However, when bred with mares of some Thoroughbred blood, his progeny displayed exceptional quality."

His offspring were known for their strength and performance-driven attributes. While not immediately tight in their front ends, these traits improved significantly with maturity, resulting in horses capable of reaching the highest levels of sport.

The Legacy of the L-Line

Ladykiller's impact extended far beyond his immediate progeny. His sons, such as Landgraf I and Lord, became foundational sires in their own right, further solidifying the prominence of the Holsteiner L-line. These stallions produced generations of champions, ensuring Ladykiller's genetic influence would shape the sport horse world for decades to come.

By 1988, Ladykiller was widely regarded as one of the most important jumper sires of modern times. His offspring consistently demonstrated the qualities necessary for success in the show jumping arena: strength, athleticism, and performance-focused conformation.

Conclusion

Ladykiller's contributions to sport horse breeding cannot be overstated. As the founder of the Holsteiner L-line, he revolutionized the breed, creating a legacy that continues to thrive today. Through his licensed sons and daughters, Ladykiller not only elevated the Holsteiner breed but also set new standards for excellence in show jumping breeding programs worldwide. His story is a testament to the transformative power of a truly exceptional stallion.

CHAPTER 5

RANTZAU

(1946–1971)

RANTZAU XX 🔵🟢
Stallion 1946 Chestnut 1.65 m
xx 276306064779046
Lic.: SF

FOXLIGHT XX 🔵🟢
xx 276306064186135
1935 Chestnut
Lic.: xx

RANCUNE XX 🔵🟢
xx
1940 Brown

FOXHUNTER XX 🔵🟢
xx 276306064482529
1929 Chestnut
Lic.: xx

CHOUIA XX 🔵🟢
xx
1925 Chestnut

CAVALIERE D'ARPINO XX 🔵🟢
xx 276306064741226
1926 Brown
Lic.: xx

ROCKELLA XX 🔵🟢
xx
1936 Chestnut

FOXLAW XX 🔵🟢
xx 1922

TRIMESTRAL XX 🔵🟢
xx 1914

SAINT JUST XX 🔵🟢
xx 1907

BARKA XX 🔵🟢
xx 1918

HAVRESAC XX 🔵🟢
xx 1915

CHUETTE XX 🔵🟢
xx 1916

BISHOP'S ROCK XX 🔵🟢
xx 1929

COQUERELLE XX 🔵🟢
xx 1924

💧 100.00% 🐴 INBREEDING COEFFICIENT

23

Rantzau, a French-bred Thoroughbred racehorse, transcended his origins to become one of the most influential sires of dressage, show jumping, and eventing horses in history. Standing at an impressive 16.1 hands, Rantzau's legacy has cemented his place as a cornerstone of the French studbook, and his influence continues to resonate in modern sport horse breeding.

From the Racetrack to Saint-Lô

Rantzau's journey to becoming a breeding legend began when Marcel Boussac sold him to the French National Stud at Saint-Lô in January 1951. Upon his arrival, he immediately caught the eye of the stud inspector, who remarked:

> "Good front extension, remarkably built through the shoulder and forearm, long haunches, this classy stallion of rare nobility also has low-placed joints and covers ground. He is high off the ground, with slightly long cannon bones and slightly straight and interiorly bony hocks; but he has a very lovely look, a good frame, good muscle tone, a well-angled shoulder, and he is well muscled."

This early assessment highlighted the qualities that would make Rantzau a transformative force in sport horse breeding—a harmonious blend of elegance, athleticism, and power.

A Prolific Breeding Career

During his two decades at stud, Rantzau covered an impressive 772 mares, averaging 38 mares per year. Between 1951 and 1962, he bred 40–49 mares annually. Though these numbers declined in the latter half of his career, his impact remained profound. It was during this period that Rantzau began to establish himself as a producer of exceptional jumping horses.

In 1958, Rantzau was ranked 17th among top show jumping producers. His influence steadily climbed in subsequent years, reaching the 11th spot in 1962 and the fifth spot in 1963. By 1964, he achieved the rank of second leading producer of show jumpers, surpassed only by the legendary Furioso.

Dominance as a Sire of Dams

Rantzau's influence extended beyond his direct offspring. In 1970, a new ranking for "best sires of dams" was introduced, with Rantzau achieving third place, following Ibrahim and Furioso. Remarkably, in the year of his death, 1971, he ascended to first place in this ranking. Although Ibrahim reclaimed the top position in 1973, Rantzau's enduring legacy was evident. Even in 1980, nine years after his death, he was ranked fourth, and in 1981, a full decade later, he once again claimed the number-one spot.

Athleticism and Sensitivity

Rantzau's offspring were known for their sensitivity and athleticism, characteristics that made them highly desirable to riders of international caliber despite their reputation for being "difficult." This combination of traits—explosive power, agility, and a sharp mind—cemented his progeny's success in elite competition and further enhanced his reputation as a sire of champions.

A Lasting Legacy

Rantzau's contributions to the world of sport horse breeding are immeasurable. His ability to produce exceptional jumpers and influential broodmares ensured his bloodlines would shape future generations of sport horses. From his early days as a racehorse to his rise as a breeding icon, Rantzau's story is one of transformation, influence, and enduring excellence.

PART II

THE FOUNDATION STALLIONS IN MODERN BREEDING

1970's - 1990's

CHAPTER 6

GALOUBET A

1972

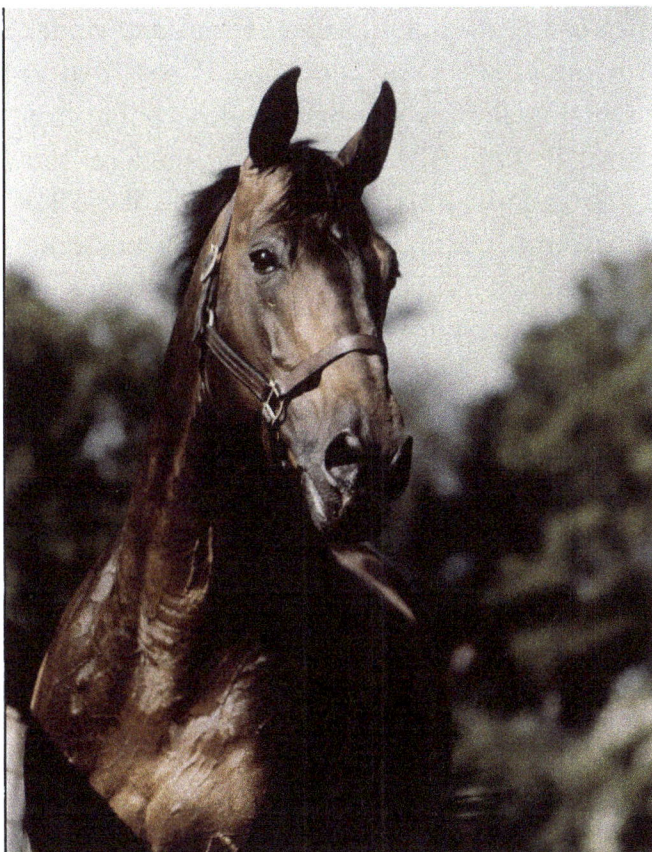

GALOUBET A 🐴✔
Stallion 1972 Brown 1.73 m
SF 25000160011039J
Lic.: AWR, SF
1.60m Jump.
Rider(s)

ALME 🐴✔
SF 25000160001122N
1966 Brown 1.66 m
Lic.: AWR, BWP, HANN, KWPN, SF
1.60m Jump.

IBRAHIM 🐴✔
SF 25000159000207P
1952 Brown 1.66 m
Lic.: SF

THE LAST ORANGE 🐴✔
SF 1941

VAILLANTE 🐴✔
SF 1943

GIRONDINE 🐴✔
SF 25000150066351C
1950 Brown 1.67 m

ULTIMATE XX 🐴✔
xx 1941

J'VINS MARS 🐴✔
SF 1931

VITI 🐴✔
Trotter 25000150024304F
1965 Chestnut

NYSTAG 🐴✔
Trotter 25000160002397C
1957 Brown
Lic.: Trotter

ABNER 🐴✔
Trotter 1944

GUSTINE 🐴✔
Trotter 1950

IDA DE BOURGOIN 🐴✔
Trotter 25000149008884Y
1952 Chestnut

BOUM III 🐴✔
Trotter 1945

CHOUQUETTE DE BOURGOIN 🐴✔
Trotter 1946

🌢 31.84% 🐎 INBREEDING COEFFICIENT

Galoubet A, Bred by Colette Lefraut and ridden by Gilles Bertran de Balanda, Galoubet A is regarded as the most pivotal stallion in the lineage descending from Ibrahim through Almé. His influence on modern showjumping breeding, particularly into the second decade of the 21st century, cannot be overstated. Among his many remarkable progeny, Baloubet du Rouet stands as his most illustrious son, yet Galoubet's legacy encompasses a lineage brimming with top-tier sport horses.

A Promising Start

Galoubet first caught the spotlight in May 1977 when competing under Benoit Mauriac. It was during this time that Gilles Bertran de Balanda, scouting for Jean-François Pellegrin, noticed the young stallion. De Balanda, however, sought a second opinion and consulted the legendary Nelson Pessoa, who surprisingly advised against purchasing Galoubet. Undeterred, Pellegrin went ahead with the acquisition, and de Balanda assumed training responsibilities.

Their collaboration soon bore fruit when the pair triumphed in the prestigious five-year-old final at Fontainebleau, establishing Galoubet as a rising star in the world of showjumping.

Competitive Achievements

By 1980, Galoubet was a formidable presence in the Nations Cups, securing victories in Aachen, Chaudefontaine, Longchamp, and Toronto, and placing second in New York. He finished eighth at the World Cup Final in Baltimore and matched this placement at the Alternative Olympic Games in Rotterdam. Despite these successes, his performance sometimes waned due to his simultaneous stud duties—a reflection of his owner's priority on breeding over competition.

In 1982, Galoubet's stellar performance at the World Championships in Dublin cemented his reputation. He was part of the gold medal-winning team and narrowly missed qualifying for the four-horse jump-off. Following this success, Pellegrin retired Galoubet to stud at the young age of ten, underscoring his strategic focus on breeding.

A Revolutionary Breeding Career

Galoubet was a trailblazer in the use of artificial insemination (AI), a practice that became legal in France in 1980. The French National Stud struck a groundbreaking deal with Pellegrin, allowing Galoubet to cover 160 mares—100 in France and 60 abroad. This innovation significantly expanded his impact on global sport horse breeding.

Over his stud career, Galoubet sired 69 approved stallions and 36 horses that competed successfully at the 1.60m level. His bloodlines have become synonymous with excellence, producing some of the most celebrated jumpers in history, including:

- **Baloubet du Rouet**: Three-time World Cup winner and an Olympic champion.
- **Quick Star**: A prolific sire and successful jumper in his own right.
- **Skippy II**: A key contributor to modern sport horse breeding.
- **Taloubet Z**: A standout performer in international competitions.

Legacy

Galoubet's influence has permeated across generations, establishing a dynasty that continues to dominate the showjumping arena. His early retirement to stud, innovative use of AI, and exceptional progeny secured his place as one of the greatest stallions in equestrian history. A true testament to the vision of his breeder, rider, and owner, Galoubet A remains a cornerstone of modern sport horse breeding.

CHAPTER 7

JALISCO B
1975

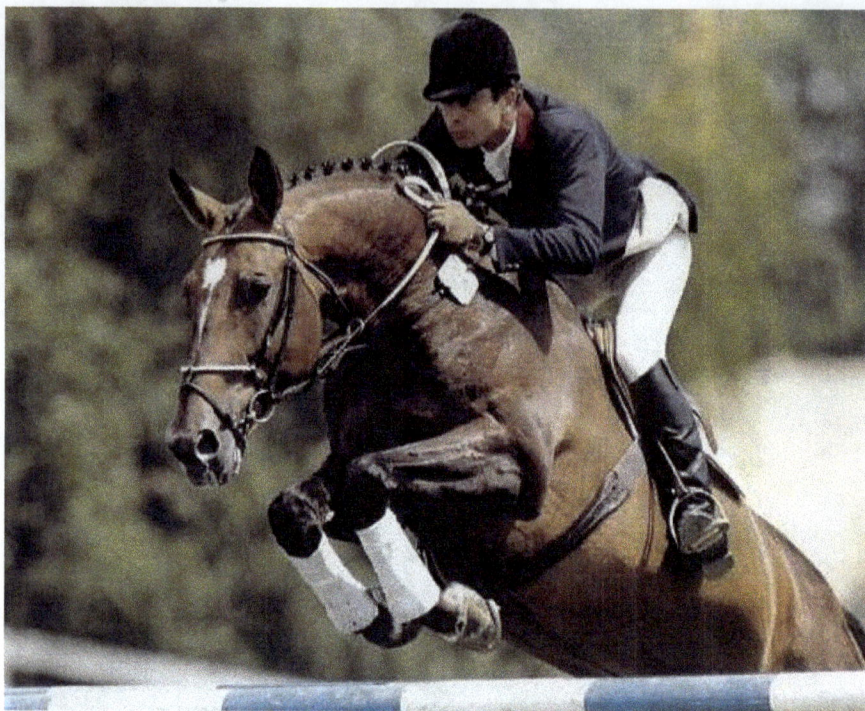

JALISCO B 🏅✅
Stallion 1975 Brown 1.74 m
SF 25000175000588W
Lic.: SF
1.60m Jump.

ALME 🏅✅
SF 25000160001122N
1966 Brown 1.66 m
Lic.: AWR, BWP, HANN, KWPN, SF
1.60m Jump.

IBRAHIM 🏅✅
SF 25000159000207P
1952 Brown 1.66 m
Lic.: SF

THE LAST ORANGE 🏅✅
SF 1941

VAILLANTE 🏅✅
SF 1943

GIRONDINE 🏅✅
SF 25000150066351C
1950 Brown 1.67 m

ULTIMATE XX 🏅✅
xx 1941

J'VINS MARS 🏅✅
SF 1931

TANAGRA 🏅✅
SF 25000150015110Z
1963 Brown

FURIOSO XX 🏅✅
xx
1939 Bay 1.66 m
Lic.: SF

PRECIPITATION XX 🏅✅
xx 1933

MAUREEN XX 🏅✅
xx 1931

DELICIEUSE 🏅✅
SF 25000149032479B
1947 Brown

JUS DE POMME 🏅✅
SF 1931

TAPISSIERE 🏅✅
SF 1941

🩸 61.72% 🐎 INBREEDING COEFFICIENT

34

Jalisco B, bred by G. Sabras, stands as a monumental figure in the world of sport horse breeding and competition. This Selle Français stallion not only left an indelible mark on the showjumping circuit but also became a cornerstone of modern equestrian breeding programs.

Ridden by Xavier Leredde, the son of the famed breeder Ferdinand Leredde, Jalisco claimed the Grand Prix of Paris in 1983, a victory that solidified his reputation as a top-tier competitor. He was also selected for the 1984 Olympic Games in Los Angeles. Unfortunately, an injury sustained on the Spanish circuit cut short his Olympic aspirations. Subsequently, he was sold to Portugal, where he continued his competitive career with Manuel Malta da Costa, representing Portugal at the 1988 Seoul Olympics.

After his stint in competition, Jalisco returned to France in 1988 to begin his breeding career. However, his breeding opportunities were somewhat limited due to the unsuitability of his semen for freezing or transport, restricting his reach to a local mare base. Despite these challenges, his impact was immense. Tragically, his career was cut short when he succumbed to colic in early 1994, at the age of 19.

A Legacy of Strength and Elasticity

Among the illustrious sons of Almé, Jalisco stood out for his physical attributes and pedigree. He was the largest of his brothers, boasting exceptional elasticity and a long stride that made him a powerhouse in the arena. His maternal lineage was impeccable; his dam, Tanagra, was the pride of Sabras breeding and consistently produced outstanding horses, including Geisha N and Danoso.

Despite these advantages, Jalisco had certain quirks. He could be a bit phlegmatic and sometimes lacked respect for obstacles. While his competitive record didn't match the dazzling heights of some of his siblings, his long-term contribution to sport horse breeding far surpassed expectations. Fifteen years after his retirement from competition, he was widely regarded as the most influential of the five best French sons of Almé.

Breeding Influence

Jalisco's influence in breeding is unparalleled. In 1982, he sired two legendary stallions: Quidam de Revel, who placed fourth at the Barcelona Olympics and became one of the world's most successful and expensive stallions, and Quito de Baussy, the 1990 World Champion. By 1995, Jalisco had achieved the number one spot on the WBFSH rankings, with eight of his progeny competing at the highest international levels. At the 1996 Olympic Games, his offspring included Rochet M, Surcouf de Revel, Vert et Rouge, and Revoulino, showcasing his enduring legacy on the global stage.

In total, Jalisco B produced 73 approved stallions and 34 horses that competed at the 1.60m level—a testament to his genetic potency and versatility.

Famous Sons and Progeny

Jalisco's list of notable offspring includes some of the most celebrated names in equestrian sports:

- **Dollar du Murier**: A world-class showjumper known for his power and precision.
- **Fuego du Prelet**: A consistent performer on the international circuit.
- **Papillon Rouge**: A legendary competitor and influential sire.

- **Quidam de Revel**: Renowned for his success at the Barcelona Olympics and his subsequent dominance as a sire.
- **Quito de Baussy**: The 1990 World Champion and a beacon of Jalisco's genetic legacy.

Legacy

Jalisco B's contributions to equestrian sports and breeding cannot be overstated. From his days in the arena to his transformative impact on Selle Français bloodlines, Jalisco's legacy endures through his remarkable progeny. His influence remains a cornerstone of modern sport horse breeding, ensuring that his name will be celebrated for generations to come.

CAPITOL I

1975

CAPITOL I ♞⊘
Stallion 1975 Grey 1.69 m
HOLST 276321210615475
Lic.: HOLST

BREEDER: HARM THORMÄHLEN, KOLLMAR

CAPITANO ♞⊘
HOLST 276321210398668
1968 Grey 1.62 m
Lic.: HESS, HOLST

FOLIA ♞⊘
HOLST 276321210460603
Hauptstutbuch
1969 Brown 1.67 m

CORPORAL ♞⊘
HOLST 276321210386463
1963 Brown
Lic.: HOLST
1.40m Jump.

RETINA ♞⊘
HOLST 276321210422403
1952 Grey 1.65 m
1.60m Jump.

MAXIMUS ♞⊘
HOLST 276321210385463
1963 Grey 1.67 m
Lic.: HOLST, SWB
1.50m Jump.

VASE ♞⊘
HOLST 276321210313703
1961 Grey 1.63 m

COTTAGE SON XX ♞⊘
xx 1944

GIMARA ♞⊘
HOLST 1948

RAMZES X ♞⊘
AA 1937
1.50m Jump.

DOLLI ♞⊘
HOLST 1945

MANOMETER XX ♞⊘
xx 1953

STOER ♞⊘
HOLST 1958

RAMZES X ♞⊘
AA 1937
1.50m Jump.

RAPPEL ♞⊘
HOLST 1939

💧 46.48% 🐎 INBREEDING COEFFICIENT

Capitol I, a towering Holsteiner stallion bred by Harm Thormählen, stands as one of the most influential sires in the history of showjumping. Despite controversy surrounding his paternal lineage—rumors suggesting Capitano might not be his sire—there is no question that Capitol's dam line is a cornerstone of Holsteiner breeding. His lineage traces back to the illustrious mare Folia, a prolific producer whose bloodlines firmly anchor Capitol's legacy.

A distinct presence, Capitol I exuded strength and power, though his conformation and appearance divided opinions. Descriptions of him highlight his imposing build:

> "A distinctive sire with plenty of stallion expression, yet lacking the final touch of charm. Large head, mighty neck with strong jowls. Top-line not ideal. Good legs with pronounced joints, but slight flaws in the transition of the joint. Relaxed, elastic gaits; enormous jumping ability."

Despite his imperfections, Capitol's performance as a sire far outshone any physical criticisms. His offspring displayed extraordinary jumping ability and athleticism, with his first crop immediately setting the tone for his legacy. Among them was **Corso**, ridden by Swiss showjumper Willi Melliger. Corso achieved significant success, claiming Grand Prix and speed class victories and competing at high-profile events such as the European Championships in St. Gallen (1987) and Rotterdam, the World Cup Final in Gothenburg (1988), and the Nations Cup at Aachen.

The early success of Capitol's progeny ignited demand for his offspring, who began setting record prices at auctions. His reputation soared as his influence spread worldwide.

A Legacy Through Stallion Sons

Capitol's line gained prominence with the licensing of three pivotal sons: **Carthago** (1987), **Cassini I** (1988), and **Cento**(1989). Each went on to leave their mark in both breeding and sport. Additionally, **Indoctro**, licensed in the Netherlands in 1990, carried Capitol's legacy into Dutch Warmblood breeding. These sons became exceptional sires in their own right, cementing Capitol's enduring influence across global sport horse breeding programs.

Capitol's impact on international showjumping became undeniable. He climbed to second place in the WBFSH rankings in 1999 and held the top position in 2000 and 2001. At the 2000 Sydney Olympic Games, Capitol was represented by three offspring: **Carthago**, **Campione M**, and **Cento**. Four years later, at the 2004 Athens Olympics, four horses carried his bloodlines: **Cardento**, **Casita**, **Cento**, and **Goliath**.

Financial and Competitive Impact

Capitol's offspring collectively earned over €5.3 million by 2007, a testament to their dominance in high-level competitions. In total, Capitol produced 57 approved stallions and 55 horses that competed at the 1.60m level, a staggering achievement that solidified his status as a breeding legend.

The Modern Influence

Although some consider Capitol's offspring slightly old-fashioned compared to the demands of modern showjumping, their presence remains unmistakable at the highest levels of the sport. His bloodlines are synonymous with scope, power, and reliability, qualities that continue to resonate with breeders and riders alike. Capitol's sons and daughters have ensured that his legacy endures, as they themselves have become prolific producers of top-tier sport horses.

Most Famous Offspring

- **Corso**: A cornerstone of Capitol's early legacy, with an illustrious competition career.
- **Cardento**: A leading sire and competitor, with consistent Olympic representation.
- **Carthago**: Known for his exceptional jumping ability and success as both a competitor and sire.
- **Cassini I**: A legend in his own right, producing numerous high-level competitors.
- **Cento**: A star competitor at the Sydney and Athens Olympics, as well as a reliable producer of top talent.
- **Indoctro**: Spread Capitol's bloodline to Dutch breeding and international sport.

Legacy

Capitol I's towering influence on showjumping is undeniable. His combination of athleticism, scope, and strong lineage made him a cornerstone of Holsteiner breeding and a sire whose legacy endures through generations. His remarkable progeny continue to shape the sport, ensuring that Capitol's name remains synonymous with excellence in modern equestrianism.

CHAPTER 9

VOLTAIRE
1979

VOLTAIRE 🟢🔵🟢
Stallion 1979 Brown 1.68 m
HANN 276331310165679
pref, WFFS-free
Lic.: BWP, HANN, KWPN, MIPAAF, OLDBG, SF
1.60m Jump.
<u>Rider(s)</u>

FURIOSO II 🔵🟢
SF 25000159040975B
1965 Chestnut 1.67 m
Lic.: BADWU, BAVAR, HANN, HESS, OLDBG, ...

GOGO MOEVE 🔵🟢
HANN 276331311332775
Hauptstutbuch
1975 Brown 1.63 m

FURIOSO XX 🔵🟢
xx
1939 Bay 1.66 m
Lic.: SF

DAME DE RANVILLE 🔵🟢
SF 25000149000368E
1947 Chestnut

GOTTHARD 🔵🟢
HANN 276331310383849
1949 Grey 1.66 m
Lic.: HANN

MOSAIK 🔵🟢
HANN 276331316992066
Hauptstutbuch
1966 Black

PRECIPITATION XX 🔵🟢
xx 1933

MAUREEN XX 🔵🟢
xx 1931

TALISMAN 🔵🟢
SF 1941

QUE JE SUIS BELLE 🔵🟢
SF 1938

GOLDFISCH II 🔵🟢
HANN 1935

AMPA 🔵🟢
HANN 1942

MORE MAGIC XX 🔵🟢
xx 1957

STUTE VON ERICH 🔵🟢
HANN 1957

💧 46.48% ⚡ INBREEDING COEFFICIENT

Voltaire, a Hanoverian bred by E. Kuwet, defied the odds to become one of the most influential sires in modern sport horse breeding. Standing just 162 cm and having a hoof defect, Voltaire faced rejection by the Oldenburg licensing commission, a verdict that could have ended his career before it began.

However, fate intervened in the form of Jan Greve, a Dutch veterinarian and passionate breeder of jumping horses, and his partner, Henk Nijhof. In the spring of 1981, while searching for a special stallion to present to the KWPN licensing, they visited Gestüt Hahnenmoor in Germany. It was there that they discovered Voltaire, and despite his physical imperfections, the pair recognized his potential.

A Temperament for Greatness

Jan Greve recalled the defining trait that set Voltaire apart:

> "Voltaire had a fantastic temperament: he was a real worker. He would sooner jump awkwardly than ever refuse a jump. That was truly a distinguishing trait and one which he passed on to his offspring."

Voltaire's willingness and determination became hallmarks of his career, both in sport and breeding.

A Promising Showjumping Career

Ridden first by E. Hendrikx and later by Jos Lansink, Voltaire demonstrated his natural athleticism and fighting spirit in the showjumping arena. Under Lansink, Voltaire achieved notable victories, including winning the Grand Prix of Berlin in 1989 and finishing second in the Grand Prix of Leeuwarden.

45

Unfortunately, during the prestigious CHIO Aachen, Voltaire sustained an injury that cut short his competitive career. Recognizing his potential as a breeding stallion, Nijhof and Greve made the decision to retire him to stud, a move that would prove transformative for the sport horse breeding industry.

A Stallion That Shaped Generations

Voltaire's influence as a sire quickly grew, solidifying his status as a foundation stallion. He produced 130 approved stallions and 107 offspring that competed at the 1.60m level in international showjumping, a remarkable achievement that highlighted his genetic contribution to the sport.

Jan Greve reflected on Voltaire's legacy:

> "Voltaire meant a lot to me. Without him, I may not have started a stud farm. He's been invaluable to the breeding industry. Perhaps he has been more influential as a dam's sire than as a direct sire. In any case, he's a true foundation stallion whom we couldn't have done without."

The Legacy Through His Offspring

Voltaire's legacy lives on through his many exceptional offspring, with several becoming household names in the equestrian world. Among his most famous progeny are:

- **Concorde**: A celebrated sire and top competitor, Concorde carried Voltaire's influence into the next generation, producing countless elite showjumpers.
- **Kannan**: One of the most sought-after stallions of modern breeding, Kannan has ranked consistently among the top sires globally. His offspring continue to dominate in international arenas.

Even more significantly, Voltaire has left a lasting imprint as a dam's sire, passing on his exceptional temperament and jumping ability to future generations. His daughters have produced some of the most successful showjumping horses of modern times.

A Foundation Stallion

Voltaire's story is one of resilience, determination, and vision. From a rejected stallion with physical limitations to a celebrated sire, he proved that greatness is not always about perfection but about heart, talent, and the ability to inspire.

For Jan Greve, Henk Nijhof, and the wider equestrian world, Voltaire was not just a stallion—he was a game-changer. His influence on breeding and sport remains profound, cementing his place among the legends of the equine world.

By the Numbers

- **Approved Stallions**: 130
- **Horses Competing at 1.60m**: 107
- **Notable Offspring**: Concorde, Kannan

Voltaire's enduring legacy is a testament to his exceptional qualities as a sire and a competitor, proving that sometimes, the smallest stallions can cast the longest shadows.

CHAPTER 10

COR DE LA BRYÈRE

1968

COR DE LA BRYERE 🔵✓
Stallion 1968 Dark brown 1.69 m
SF 25000160011506B
Lic.: HOLST, SF

BREEDER: THERÈSE ESSAYAN, YVRE-LE-POLIN, FR

RANTZAU XX 🔵✓
xx 276306064779046
1946 Chestnut 1.65 m
Lic.: SF

QUENOTTE 🔵✓
SF 25000150003047L
1960 Brown 1.70 m

FOXLIGHT XX 🔵✓
xx 276306064186135
1935 Chestnut
Lic.: xx

RANCUNE XX 🔵✓
xx
1940 Brown

LURIOSO 🔵✓
SF 25000159001698T
1955 Brown 1.64 m
Lic.: SF

VESTALE DU BOIS MARGOT 🔵✓
SF 25000149001674K
1942 Chestnut

FOXHUNTER XX 🔵✓
xx 1929

CHOUIA XX 🔵✓
xx 1925

CAVALIERE D'ARPINO XX 🔵✓
xx 1926

ROCKELLA XX 🔵✓
xx 1936

FURIOSO XX 🔵✓
xx 1939

RIQUETTE 🔵✓
SF 1939

LANDAU 🔵✓
SF 1933

KRISTINE DU BOIS MARGOT 🔵✓
SF 1932

💧 67.19% 🐎 INBREEDING COEFFICIENT

49

Cor de la Bryère, affectionately nicknamed "Cord," is widely regarded as one of the most influential stallions in the history of jumping horse breeding. Born in 1968 and bred by Thérèse Essayan in France, Cor de la Bryère became a cornerstone of modern sport horse breeding, particularly in Holstein. Known for his exceptional technique and his ability to pass on flawless form over jumps, Cor de la Bryère's name is revered by breeders and riders alike, especially when found on the mare line.

Regal Pedigree

Cor de la Bryère's pedigree was a testament to excellence. His sire is the great **Rantzau**. His dam **Quenotte** by **Lurioso** was by Furioso, who left an indelible mark on French jumping horse breeding. Furioso was the sire of Lutteur B, the 1964 Olympic gold medalist with Pierre Jonquères d'Oriola, and Pomone B, the world showjumping champion of 1968.

An Unexpected Journey

Remarkably, Cor de la Bryère almost didn't make it to the breeding shed. In 1970, the Haras du Pin selection committee dismissed him, stating that he was "too much of a sport horse" and suggesting he be gelded for use as a riding horse. This near oversight could have cost the equestrian world one of its most influential sires.

Fortunately, Cor de la Bryère's story took a different turn when he was purchased in 1971 by the Holsteiner Verband and imported to Schleswig-Holstein, Germany. That same year, he triumphed at the 100-day stallion performance test, becoming champion and immediately drawing attention to his potential as a breeding stallion.

A Perfect Match for Holstein

Bernard le Courtois, a prominent French equestrian journalist, highlighted Cor de la Bryère's unique influence:

> "Some stallions cross very well in a particular situation. Cor de la Bryère was exceptional in the 70s in Holstein because he was a horse that was very quick with the front legs. He didn't have the power on the back side, but he was very electric, with the blood of the Thoroughbred, Rantzau. Mixed with the heavy Holsteiner mares, he was fantastic. But when we tried to breed Cor de la Bryère with the French mares, we had rabbits. Cor de la Bryère needed a very strong mare, and we didn't have this kind of mare in France."

In Holstein, Cor de la Bryère transformed the breeding program. His bloodlines, when paired with the substantial and powerful Holsteiner mares, created a perfect synergy, producing horses with elegance, speed, and exceptional technique over jumps.

A Legacy of Champions

Cor de la Bryère's influence extends through his direct offspring and many subsequent generations. He sired **113 approved stallions** and **34 horses that competed at the 1.60m level**, leaving an unparalleled legacy in the world of sport horse breeding.

Most Famous Sons and Grandsons:

- **Caletto I**: Known for his elegance and outstanding jumping ability.
- **Contender**: A stallion who became a legend in his own right, producing countless international showjumpers and dressage horses.

- **Cantus**: A sire of champions who passed on exceptional power and scope.
- **Calvaro Z**: A top competitor on the international stage.
- **Corland VDL**: Renowned for his technique and success as a sire.
- **Corrado**: A prolific producer of top-level showjumpers with immense scope.
- **Calvados**: Known for passing on his athleticism and intelligence.
- **Cash**: An influential sire with a competitive edge.
- **Bacardi VDL**: A modern-day representative of the Cor de la Bryère lineage.
- **Clinton**: A stalwart in modern showjumping breeding.

Revolutionizing Modern Breeding

Cor de la Bryère's legacy is not just in his offspring but in the way he transformed sport horse breeding. His ability to refine and improve Holsteiner lines has had a ripple effect across the equestrian world. Breeders continue to seek his influence, especially through his presence in the mare lines, where his traits of quick reflexes, elasticity, and exceptional jumping form are most evident.

By the Numbers

- **Approved Stallions**: 113
- **Horses Competing at 1.60m**: 34

Legacy

Cor de la Bryère was more than just a stallion—he was a revolution. From being nearly dismissed in France to becoming the foundation of modern Holsteiner breeding, his story is one of perseverance, vision, and unmatched influence. His name remains a hallmark of quality, ensuring his place among the legends of equine history.

CHAPTER 11

CONTENDER

1984

CONTENDER 🔵🟢
Stallion 1984 Dark brown 1.70 m
HOLST 276321210023884
Lic.: AWR, HANN, HOLST, KWPN, OLDBG, RHEIN

BREEDER: NIKO DETLEF, FEHMARN

CALYPSO II 🔵🟢
HOLST 276321210610574
1974 Dark brown 1.75 m
Lic.: HANN, HOLST
1.45m Jump.

GOFINE 🔵🟢
HOLST 276321210523770
Hauptstutbuch
1970 Brown 1.62 m

COR DE LA BRYERE 🔵🟢
SF 25000160011506B
1968 Dark brown 1.69 m
Lic.: HOLST, SF

TABELLE 🔵🟢
HOLST 276321210292103
1959 Brown 1.65 m

RAMIRO Z 🔵🟢
HOLST 276321210389565
pref
1965 Dark brown 1.75 m
Lic.: BWP, HANN, HOLST, KWPN, NRPS, SF, W...
1.60m Jump.

CITA 🔵🟢
HOLST 276321210387303
1966 Brown 1.64 m

RANTZAU XX 🔵🟢
xx 1946

QUENOTTE 🔵🟢
SF 1960

HEISSPORN 🔵🟢
HOLST 1940

HYAZINTHE 🔵🟢
HOLST 1949

RAIMOND 🔵🟢
HOLST 1960

VALINE 🔵🟢
HOLST 1961
1.50m Jump.

LADYKILLER XX 🔵🟢
xx 1961

ROMINA 🔵🟢
HOLST 1957

💧 42.38% 🐎 INBREEDING COEFFICIENT

55

Contender, one of the most remarkable Holsteiner stallions in history, passed away in January 2014, just shy of his 30th birthday. He solidified his place as the most influential son of **Calypso II** and an exceptional descendant of the legendary **Cor de la Bryère**. Contender's impact on sport horse breeding spans decades, with his bloodlines continuing to shape the future of equestrian sport.

A Stallion of Exceptional Class

Dr. Thomas Nissen, Gabriele Pochhammer, Donata von Preußen, and Joachim Tietz captured Contender's essence in *The Holsteiner Horse*:

> "An important stud stallion with fantastic lines, great expression and charm. All in all, a stud stallion of exceptional class: first-class conformation with very well-balanced paces and good rhythm, whereby he could have had a more ground-covering walk and a more pronounced flank. Outstanding jumping ability, as could be expected, considering his genes, very good style and technique."

While Contender's early offspring in Holstein didn't immediately turn heads, breeders in Oldenburg quickly recognized his potential. It became evident over time that **Contender worked best with mares carrying a high percentage of Thoroughbred blood**, which brought out his ability to pass on athleticism and refinement.

A Journey Through Breeding

Contender's journey to prominence began under unusual circumstances. As **Norbert Boley**, the manager of the Holstein Verband, recounted in an interview with *Z Magazine*, Contender's early years included a stint in Oldenburg:

"I bought Contender as a foal. Eventually, he was brought to the selection, and halfway through his performance, Klatte from Oldenburg expressed his interest in the stallion over a pint of beer. Things developed so enthusiastically with a number of studbook people that Klatte already believed he had bought the stallion, while I, the authorized person, did not know anything about it. When I learned one day later that Klatte genuinely believed he was the new owner, I did not send him away just like that. Never treat your clients with disrespect – at least not when they act in good faith. We talked about it and came to a compromise. The stallion was leased to Oldenburg for three years."

During his time in Oldenburg, Contender earned widespread acclaim, winning the **1987 Adelheidsdorf stallion performance test** with a remarkable jumping index of **146.6**. He was also named the 1-b main premium vice-champion in Oldenburg, based on his excellent first crop of foals.

Breeding Excellence

Contender's dam, **Gofine**, reflected the rich heritage of the Haseldorfer Marsh, with a pedigree that included **Ramiro**, **Ladykiller xx**, and other influential stallions from the Holsteiner lineage. Gofine's line carried the strength and versatility necessary to complement Contender's genetics.

As Contender's fame grew, his offspring became highly sought after. By 2000, the Holsteiner Board limited his breeding to registered Holsteiner mares to preserve the exclusivity of his bloodlines.

By the Numbers

Contender's breeding career was nothing short of extraordinary:

- **194 Approved Stallions**: A testament to his ability to pass on desirable traits.
- **59 State Premium Mares**: Including Riconda, the Elite Mare Show winner at Rastede in 1993.
- **110 Horses Competing at 1.60m Level**: A measure of his impact on international showjumping.
- **498 Successful Offspring in Sport**: Across various levels and disciplines.

Famous Offspring

Contender's legacy lives on through his celebrated progeny, many of whom have reached the highest levels of international competition:

- **Chellano Z**: A top sire who has influenced modern sport horse breeding.
- **Con Air**: Known for his elegance and scope in jumping.
- **Montender**: A double gold medalist at the 2005 European Championships.
- **Checkmate**: A consistent performer in international showjumping.
- **Chiara**: A top-level competitor with numerous Grand Prix wins.

Revolutionizing Modern Breeding

Contender's success reshaped the landscape of showjumping breeding. His ability to consistently produce offspring with exceptional jumping ability, rideability, and conformation earned him a reputation as one of the most sought-after stallions of his time. His influence can be seen not only in his direct offspring but also in the generations of sport horses that trace back to his bloodlines.

Legacy

Contender's story is one of perseverance and excellence. From his early years to his lasting impact on the breeding world, he remains a legend in equestrian history. As one of the greatest stallions to descend from **Cor de la Bryère**, Contender's legacy endures, shaping the future of sport horse breeding and ensuring his place among the giants of the Holsteiner lineage.

CHAPTER 12

∽

LANDGRAF I
1966

LANDGRAF I ⊕⊘
Stallion 1966 Dark brown 1.70 m
HOLST 276321210391966
Lic.: HOLST

LADYKILLER XX ⊕⊘
xx 276306064000861
1961 Brown 1.64 m
Lic.: HOLST, xx

SAILING LIGHT XX ⊕⊘
xx 276306064006849
1949 Chestnut
Lic.: xx

BLUE PETER XX ⊕⊘
xx 1936

SOLAR CYGNET XX ⊕⊘
xx 1940

LONE BEECH XX ⊕⊘
xx 276306064953839
1939 Brown

LOANINGDALE XX ⊕⊘
xx 1929

FARTUCH XX ⊕⊘
xx 1932

WARTHBURG ⊕⊘
HOLST 276321210320903
Hauptstutbuch
1962 Brown 1.67 m

ALDATO ⊕⊘
HOLST 276321210377658
1958 Dark brown 1.67 m
Lic.: HOLST, HSH

ANBLICK XX ⊕⊘
xx 1938

KRETA ⊕⊘
HOLST 1951

SCHNEENELKE ⊕⊘
HOLST 276321210284503
1958 Brown 1.63 m

FANGBALL ⊕⊘
HOLST 1946

BLUEMCHEN ⊕⊘
HOLST 1943

🜄 63.48% 🐎 INBREEDING COEFFICIENT

Landgraf I, a Holsteiner stallion born in 1966, revolutionized showjumping breeding and established himself as one of the most influential stallions in equestrian history. Despite a challenging start, his legacy endures, with his bloodlines continuing to dominate the modern sport horse scene.

Early Challenges and Breakthrough

Landgraf I was sired by **Ladykiller xx**, a Thoroughbred stallion whose progeny marked a turning point in Holsteiner breeding. His dam, **Warthburg**, from the prestigious Stem 275, contributed valuable performance genes from **Ethelbert**, **Achill**, and **Cicero**, laying the foundation for the modern Holsteiner sport horse.

Landgraf was licensed in 1968, finishing 5th out of twelve sons of Ladykiller xx. The licensing committee described him as:

> "A stallion with a lot of presence, good gaits with excellent propulsion, good conformation, and average hindquarters."

Despite his promise, Landgraf was nearly lost to Holstein. Initially stationed at Haselau, where breeders favored his sire, Ladykiller xx, Landgraf attracted few mares. In 1970, the Holstein Association Board decided to sell him to Hans Dussler in Baden-Württemberg.

His breakthrough came in 1975 at **Equitana** in Germany, where Landgraf cleared a 6'6" jump with ease, captivating international riders and sparking interest in his offspring.

Conformation and Temperament

Landgraf I was renowned for his imposing appearance and exceptional temperament. He was described as having:

- A beautiful face with expressive eyes.
- A long, broad neck and a smooth topline.
- A muscular croup and strong bone structure.
- Slight conformation faults, including being sickle-hocked as a youth, which straightened with age, and issues in the hind fetlocks.

While his offspring sometimes inherited his hind leg faults, they nearly always inherited his jumping talent, type, and striking facial features.

Phenomenal Performance and Progeny

Landgraf's progeny were late bloomers, often appearing leggy and narrow in youth but maturing into exceptional athletes. His offspring were known for their:

- Tremendous jumping ability, often starting awkwardly but improving with maturity.
- Careful and talented jumping style, with tight front legs and excellent bascule.
- Versatility and competitiveness in international showjumping.

In total, Landgraf's progeny earned over **€4.5 million** in prize money, with 35 horses competing at the **1.60m level** and **161 approved stallions**.

Dominance in Global Breeding

Landgraf I's influence on global breeding is unparalleled. According to Bernard le Courtois, in the **2007–2008 edition of Monneron**, Landgraf was one of the four dominant male lines, alongside **Almé**, **Cor de la Bryère**, and **Capitol**.

Landgraf sired five stallions in the top 75 world rankings, including:

- **Burggraaf**: Ranked 6th, with 26 winners.
- **Libero H**: Ranked 9th, with 22 CSI winners, including a World Cup victory.
- **Lavall I**: Known for producing athletic offspring with power and scope.
- **Lacrimoso**: A top international showjumper.

Lasting Impact

Landgraf I's genetic contribution is seen in sport horses worldwide, making him a cornerstone of modern breeding. His ability to pass on exceptional jumping talent, coupled with his versatility and temperament, has ensured his place as one of the most celebrated stallions in history.

Legacy

Despite early skepticism, Landgraf I rose to become a legend in showjumping breeding. His legacy is immortalized in the extraordinary success of his offspring, whose achievements on the international stage continue to cement his status as the "King of Modern Showjumping Breeding."

CHAPTER 13

NARCOS II

1979

NARCOS II 🔵🟤🟢
Stallion 1979 Bay 1.70 m
SF 25000179297317N
Stb.
Lic.: AAFE, BH, BWP, CDE, ISH, KWPN, SBS, SF, SVH
1.60m Jump.

FAIR PLAY III 🟤🟢
SF 25000160004178R
1971 Brown
Lic.: SF

QUASTOR 🟤🟢
SF 25000160003410B
1960 Brown 1.65 m
Lic.: SF

IBRAHIM 🟤🟢
SF 1952

LA CITADELLE 🟤🟢
SF 1955

MA POMME 🟤🟢
SF 25000150065729D
1956 Brown 1.66 m

FURIOSO XX 🟤🟢
xx 1939

HARMONIE 🟤🟢
SF 1951

GEMINI 🟤🟢
SF 25000150215800H
1972 Chestnut

TANAEL 🟤🟢
SF 25000160003412Z
1963 Chestnut 1.66 m
Lic.: SF

IBRAHIM 🟤🟢
SF 1952

KADINE 🟤🟢
SF 1954

IL PLEUT BERGERE 🟤🟢
SF 25000150066518W
1952 Chestnut 1.65 m

FOUDROYANT II XX 🟤🟢
xx 1938

VERGONNE 🟤🟢
SF 1943

💧 49.22% 🐴 INBREEDING COEFFICIENT

Narcos II, a Selle Français stallion bred by Jean Brohier, epitomized excellence in both performance and breeding. Born and raised at the Brohier family stud, Narcos II was the culmination of generations of careful selection and became one of the most celebrated showjumping stallions in the world.

Early Career: A Champion in the Making

Narcos II's career began with brilliance, showcasing his talent as a young horse. With Denis Brohier as his first rider, Narcos II quickly established himself as a rising star. He achieved the following milestones at Fontainebleau:

- **3rd place** in the 4-year-old championships.
- **1st place** in the 5-year-old championships with Éric Navet.
- **1st place** in the 6-year-old championships, again under Éric Navet's guidance.

These successes laid the foundation for his exceptional international career.

International Success

Under Éric Navet, Narcos II quickly became a formidable force in showjumping. He represented France in Nations Cup competitions and contributed to victories in:

- **Madrid**
- **Luxembourg**
- **Lucerne**
- **Rome**
- **Hickstead**
- **St. Gallen**
- **Aachen**

- **Calgary**
- **La Baule**

Narcos II also competed in the USA, further cementing his reputation as an international star.

Adversity and Comeback

In 1987, Narcos II faced a major setback when he was sidelined by laminitis. The condition forced him out of competition for two years. Despite this, he made a remarkable recovery, returning to compete at the national level.

In 1994, Narcos II, ridden by Florian Angot, added another highlight to his career, winning the **European Junior Championship**.

In total, Narcos II amassed:

- **178 victories**
- **567 placings**
- Winnings of **2,420,646 francs**

Legacy in Breeding

Narcos II's influence extended far beyond the competition arena. As a sire, he left an indelible mark on showjumping breeding, producing **82 approved stallions** and **18 horses competing at the 1.60m level**.

His most famous offspring include:

- **Kouros d'Helby**: A star with Éric Février in international competitions.
- **Tangelo van de Zuuthoeve**: A highly influential stallion in Belgium.

- **Hold Up Premier**: Known for his exceptional pedigree and performance.
- **Twist du Vallon**: Named Horse of the Year in 1998 in the USA with Ward McLain.
- **Viking du Tillard**: Champion of France in 1996 with Hervé Godignon.

Other notable descendants include:

- **Urbain du Monnai** ridden by Roger-Yves Bost.
- **Tisca** ridden by Gilles Bertran de Balanda.
- **Une des Cresles** ridden by Patrick Martin.
- **Ulanne du Plessis** ridden by Annick Chenu.
- **Anisette Brécéenne** ridden by Bruno Rocuet.
- **Altesse de Boêle** ridden by Patrick Martin.

Narcos II's progeny not only excelled in performance but also inherited his remarkable temperament, athleticism, and versatility.

Representation Worldwide

Narcos II's legacy thrives internationally, with several of his sons gaining popularity:

- **Hold Up Premier**: A standout in Holland, descended from a Quidam de Revel mare.
- **Hinault**: Out of a Landgraf mare, also representing his bloodlines in Holland.
- **Tangelo van de Zuuthoeve**: Extremely popular in Belgium for his consistent ability to pass on quality and athleticism.

Legacy

Narcos II remains a cornerstone of modern showjumping breeding. His remarkable achievements, resilience in the face of adversity, and unparalleled influence as a sire have immortalized him in the annals of equestrian history. His legacy continues to shine through his descendants, making him a symbol of French equestrian excellence.

CHAPTER 14

NIMMERDOR

1972

NIMMERDOR 🔵✓
Stallion 1972 Brown 1.68 m
KWPN 147STB-H
pref, Stb.
Lic.: HOLST, KWPN, SF
1.60m Jump.

FARN 🔵✓ HOLST 276321210378459 pref 1959 Brown 1.69 m Lic.: HOLST, KWPN	**FAX I** 🔵✓ HOLST 276321210372054 1954 Brown 1.62 m Lic.: HOLST	**FANATIKER** 🔵✓ HOLST 1940	
		MARGOT 🔵✓ HOLST 1938	
	DORETTE 🔵✓ HOLST 276321210269603 Hauptstutbuch 1945 Black 1.56 m	**MONARCH** 🔵✓ HOLST 1941	
		SCHELLE 🔵✓ HOLST 1940	
RAMONAA 🔵✓ NWP 187Bv ster 1963 Brown	**KORIDON XX** 🔵✓ xx BB1901 1946 Chestnut 1.64 m Lic.: Sprt, xx	**KARAMONT XX** 🔵✓ xx 1939	
		POUTZI XX 🔵✓ xx 1934	
	FRIEDHILDE II 🔵✓ NWP 33693B pref 1958 Chestnut 1.63 m	**SENATOR** 🔵✓ NWP 1953	
		FRIEDHILDE 🔵✓ NWP 1945	

💧 35.55% 🐎 INBREEDING COEFFICIENT

Nimmerdor, a Holsteiner stallion bred by VDL Stud, revolutionized modern sport horse breeding and established himself as one of the most influential sires in equestrian history. His story intertwines with that of Wiepke van der Lageweg, the man who transformed from a cattle dealer into one of the world's premier stallion breeders, thanks to this remarkable horse.

A Star is Born

Nimmerdor was born in June 1972, the same month Wiepke van der Lageweg purchased his first horse—a prophetic coincidence that would define both their futures. Three years later, Wiepke recognized Nimmerdor's potential and purchased him from breeder J.A. Dijkstra of Woudsend for 25,000 florins, a significant sum at the time. This investment would lay the foundation for Wiepke's rise to prominence in the equestrian world.

Performance Test and Early Career

In 1975, Nimmerdor excelled in his performance test, particularly in jumping, though his character earned only a score of 7 due to his demanding temperament. Under Bert Romp and later Albert Voorn, Nimmerdor competed internationally in Berlin, Paris, Gothenburg, Dortmund, and London.

He was selected for the **1984 Los Angeles Olympics**, but Wiepke decided to prioritize Nimmerdor's breeding career instead, a decision that proved transformative for the sport horse world.

Albert Voorn's Tribute

Albert Voorn, who partnered with Nimmerdor during the early stages of his career, reminisced about the stallion's extraordinary talent:

> "Even now after all those years, there is hardly a day that I don't think of Nimmerdor. He was one of the most talented horses I ever rode. His carefulness combined with his great abilities and scope is seldom seen in a horse... If I'd had him now, he would be very hard to beat. Nimmerdor was the better horse, no doubt!"

(Excerpt from Claartje van Andel's tribute in *Breeding News*, June 2003)

Influence on Breeding

After his international career, Nimmerdor became a cornerstone of global sport horse breeding. He was the sire of **73 approved stallions** and **37 horses competing at the 1.60m level**, spreading his influence across continents.

KWPN Approved Sons and Grandsons

Among his 18 KWPN-approved sons were:

- **Ahorn**
- **Wellington**
- **Goodtimes**
- **Heartbreaker** (his most famous son)

His legacy continued through **39 KWPN-approved grandsons**, including:

- **Emilion**
- **Farrington**
- **Glennridge**

- **Kalusha**
- **Matterhorn**
- **Ohorn**
- **Pacific**
- **Sydney**

Globally, Nimmerdor sired over 40 approved stallions and countless national and international jumping horses. His ability to pass on his scope, athleticism, and carefulness made him an invaluable asset to breeders.

Recognition and Legacy

In recognition of his profound influence on sport horse breeding, Nimmerdor was awarded the prestigious "Preferent" predicate by the KWPN. In 2000, he was named **"Stallion of the Century"** in the Netherlands, cementing his place in history.

Even in retirement, his owner, Wiepke van der Lageweg, believed in Nimmerdor's relevance to modern breeding:

> "Nimmerdor could come back tomorrow and have a lot of work. He was unbelievable… but now we need more blood for today's fences and distances, though we always need scope."

Retirement and Passing

In March 1999, Nimmerdor was retired from breeding to enjoy his final years. He passed away on April 25, 2003, at the remarkable age of 31, leaving behind a legacy that continues to shape the sport horse world.

Most Famous Son: Heartbreaker

Among his many exceptional offspring, **Heartbreaker** stands out as Nimmerdor's crowning achievement. Heartbreaker became a foundational sire in his own right, further extending Nimmerdor's influence into subsequent generations of elite showjumpers.

Legacy

Nimmerdor's legacy transcends his remarkable career and extends to the lasting impact he made on sport horse breeding. As a competitor, he dazzled; as a sire, he transformed the breeding landscape. His influence is seen not only in his direct descendants but in the ongoing excellence of sport horses worldwide, ensuring his place as a true icon in equestrian history.

CHAPTER 15

∞

CLOVER HILL

1973

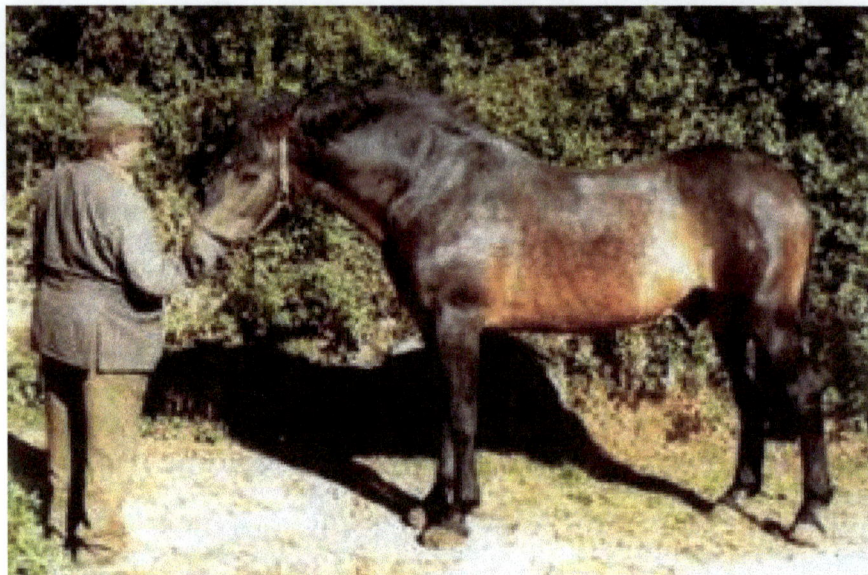

		ARCTIC STORM XX 🔵🟢	ARCTIC STAR XX 🔵🟢
		xx	xx 1942
		1959 Brown	
	GOLDEN BEAKER XX 🔵🟢	Lic.: xx	RABINA XX 🔵🟢
	xx IHR12785		xx 1939
	1965 Chestnut		
	Lic.: xx		PRECIPTIC XX 🔵🟢
		CORBALLY PRINCESS XX 🔵🟢	xx 1942
CLOVER HILL 🔵🟢		xx	
Stallion 1973 Brown 1.73 m		1954 Brown	WHIRLING DUN XX 🔵🟢
ISH IHR17310			xx 1934
Lic.: ISH, RID			
		TARA 🔵🟢	FOREST HERO 🔵🟢
		RID 16047	RID 1936
	BY TARA 🔵🟢	1943 Grey	
	ISH	Lic.: ISH	UNION HALL 🔵🟢
			RID 0
			Missing
		ADD DAM	
			Missing

💧 53.91% 🐎 INBREEDING COEFFICIENT

Clover Hill, an Irish Sport Horse (ISH), is widely regarded as one of the most influential foundation stallions in the Irish Studbook. Bred by Matt Page, this remarkable stallion never left the stud farm where he was born, yet his legacy has spanned generations and impacted sport horse breeding on a global scale.

Breeding and Pedigree

Clover Hill was sired by the Thoroughbred stallion **Golden Beaker** out of a mare from strong Irish Draught lines. Registered as an Irish Sport Horse, Clover Hill embodied the ideal combination of Thoroughbred refinement and Irish Draught strength. His progeny inherited his trademark courage, athleticism, and scope, qualities that established him as a cornerstone of Irish sport horse breeding.

A Singular Personality

Clover Hill's influence extended far beyond his genetic contributions—his story is as much about his owner's quirks as his own talents. The owner, a colorful character in the Irish equestrian world, famously kept Clover Hill's stud fee consistent throughout his career. However, securing a covering from the stallion was no guarantee. Decisions were based not on the mare's merit, but on the owner's mood: whether he liked the mare's owner, their car, horsebox, or even the vibe of the day. Stories abound of breeders driving hours to the stud, only to be turned away for reasons as enigmatic as the man himself.

Despite these eccentricities, Clover Hill's progeny proved so exceptional that breeders were willing to gamble on the owner's whims for a chance to produce foals with his legendary bloodlines.

Traits and Impact

Clover Hill stamped his offspring with a distinctive set of traits that made them highly sought after:

- **Scopey Jumpers**: His progeny possessed exceptional jumping ability, capable of excelling in the most challenging international arenas.
- **Bravery**: Clover Hill horses were known for their fearless approach to fences, a critical quality in top-level showjumping.
- **Stubbornness and Difficulty**: While talented, many of his offspring were also described as "difficult" or "stubborn," requiring skilled riders to unlock their potential.

These traits, coupled with his ability to pass on his athleticism and performance capabilities, made Clover Hill a defining stallion in the Irish Sport Horse breeding program.

Achievements in Breeding

Clover Hill's contribution to the Irish Studbook is unparalleled. Over his breeding career, he produced:

- **37 Approved Stallions**: These sons carried his bloodlines into the next generation, further cementing his legacy in sport horse breeding.
- **38 Horses Competing at 1.60m**: His progeny excelled at the highest levels of international showjumping, showcasing the talent and versatility that became synonymous with the Clover Hill name.

Legacy

Clover Hill's influence has endured long after his passing in 1997. As a foundation stallion, his bloodlines are woven into the fabric of modern Irish Sport Horse breeding. His progeny and descendants continue to excel in disciplines ranging from showjumping to eventing, representing the best of Irish breeding on the world stage.

His legacy is a testament to the power of exceptional genetics, as well as the enduring appeal of Irish Sport Horses in equestrian sports. Clover Hill may never have left his birthplace, but his impact has traveled far and wide, securing his place as a legend in the annals of equestrian history.

CHAPTER 16

❧

CAVALIER ROYALE
1978

CAVALIER ROYALE ⚥✔
Stallion 1978 Black 1.72 m
HOLST 276321210298678
Lic.: ISH, WSI

COR DE LA BRYERE ⚥✔
SF 25000160011506B
1968 Dark brown 1.69 m
Lic.: HOLST, SF

RANTZAU XX ⚥✔
xx 276306064779046
1946 Chestnut 1.65 m
Lic.: SF

FOXLIGHT XX ⚥✔
xx 1935

RANCUNE XX ⚥✔
xx 1940

QUENOTTE ⚥✔
SF 25000150003047L
1960 Brown 1.70 m

LURIOSO ⚥✔
SF 1955

VESTALE DU BOIS MARGOT ⚥✔
SF 1942

LIGUSTRA ⚥✔
HOLST 276321211006974
Staatsprämle
1974 Brown 1.68 m

LIGUSTER ⚥✔
HOLST 276321210403470
1970 Brown
Lic.: HOLST

LANDSTURM ⚥✔
HOLST 1966

AUMINA ⚥✔
HOLST 1964

DAMIRA ⚥✔
HOLST 276321210408467
Hauptstutbuch
1967 Dark brown 1.61 m

COLOMBO ⚥✔
HOLST 1960

ZAMORA ⚥✔
HOLST 1963

💧 51.95% 🐎 INBREEDING COEFFICIENT

Cavalier Royale, a Holsteiner stallion bred by A. Johanssen, became one of the most transformative sires in Ireland's equestrian history. His remarkable career as a breeding stallion challenged the dominance of Clover Hill, who had long been considered the greatest sire in Ireland. Cavalier Royale not only rivaled Clover Hill's influence but redefined excellence in sport horse breeding with his exceptional offspring.

Breeding and Early Promise

Cavalier Royale's pedigree is rooted in top Holsteiner bloodlines, which he brought to Ireland when he was imported to stand at stud. With his striking good looks, impeccable temperament, and natural athleticism, Cavalier Royale quickly established himself as a game-changer in the Irish Sport Horse (ISH) breeding program.

His dominance in Ireland began in 1993, when his first crop of three-year-olds made waves at the **Millstreet National Championships**, also known as the Young Irelander. Out of 500 stallions in Ireland capable of producing qualifiers for the Young Horse National Championships, Cavalier Royale stood out. Eight of his three-year-old progeny qualified for the Millstreet finals, with five advancing to the prestigious Saturday night final session. Cavalier Royale finished with:

- **Champion**: Magnetic
- **5th Place Finalist**
- **9th Place Finalist**

This unprecedented success firmly established Cavalier Royale as a leading sire in Ireland, capable of producing consistent winners at the highest level of young horse competition.

Impact on Breeding

Cavalier Royale left an indelible mark on the Irish breeding industry:

- **Quality Stamping**: His offspring were renowned for their beauty, athleticism, and temperament. Regardless of the dam, they inherited Cavalier Royale's exceptional movement, jumping ability, and reliability.
- **Color Consistency**: Approximately 65% of his offspring were seal brown like himself, with 35% bay, and only occasional greys—never chestnuts.
- **Crossbreeding Excellence**: He transmitted more blood and quality than expected, making him ideal for average half-bred mares and improving their progeny dramatically.

Breeders often praised Cavalier Royale for producing foals that were naturally gifted jumpers, even when paired with mares of varying quality. His progeny dominated Ireland's young horse championships for years, a testament to his prepotency as a sire.

International Success

Following early agitation from breeders, Cavalier Royale was officially upgraded in 1997 after blood tests confirmed he was the sire of **Amos**, François Mathy's European showjumping star. Originally named Tisscrum Cavalier, Amos won the **West Coast Grand Prix** with Rich Fellers before returning to Europe to compete successfully.

Cavalier Royale's influence reached far beyond Ireland. His offspring excelled on the international stage, particularly in the United States, where top competitors included:

- **McGuinness**: Ridden by Rich Fellers, McGuinness ranked second on the US standings in 2004, earning $144,348 and placing in 18 competitions, including the **Shell Derby Cup in Calgary** and the **Del Mar Grand Prix**.

- **Cameron Hills Shanroe**
- **La Dona**
- **Bantry Bay**
- **Shannondale Truman**

Cavalier Royale's progeny continued to shine, achieving top placings in Grand Prix events and demonstrating the enduring power of his bloodlines.

Sporting Career

Cavalier Royale himself had a promising career as an international showjumper before a hock injury curtailed his performance. A Puissance winner with a remarkable leap of 7'3", Cavalier Royale proved his own athleticism and bravery, qualities he passed on to his offspring.

Achievements as a Sire

Cavalier Royale's contribution to breeding is extraordinary:

- **21 Approved Stallions**: His sons carried forward his legacy, ensuring his influence would endure for generations.
- **57 Horses Competing at 1.60m**: Cavalier Royale's progeny reached the pinnacle of international showjumping, a testament to his reliability as a sire of world-class performers.

Notable Offspring

Some of Cavalier Royale's most famous progeny include:

- **HHS Calais**: A standout competitor and influential sire.
- **Chippison**: Another exceptional jumper who inherited his sire's athleticism and temperament.

Legacy

Cavalier Royale's ability to consistently produce winners at both young horse championships and the highest levels of international competition secured his place as one of the most significant sires in Ireland's history. His impact on the Irish Sport Horse breeding program rivaled that of Clover Hill, proving that his bloodlines were nothing short of transformational.

Even decades after his passing in 1999, Cavalier Royale's name remains synonymous with quality, athleticism, and success. His legacy endures through his progeny and their ongoing contributions to the sport horse world, ensuring that Cavalier Royale will forever be celebrated as a legend in equestrian breeding.

CHAPTER 17

DARCO
1980

DARCO 🐴✓
Stallion 1980 Dark brown 1.66 m
BWP 056002W00001387
BWP_Ambassadeur
Lic.: AWR, BWP, HOLST, KWPN, NRPS, OLDBC
1.60m Jump.
Rider(s)

LUGANO VAN LA ROCHE 🐴✓
HANN 276331314502663
BWP_Ambassadeur
1963 Chestnut 1.63 m
Lic.: BWP, HANN

OCOUCHA 🐴✓
BWP 056002W00014829
Stb.
1968 Dark brown

LUGANO I 🐴✓
HANN 276331310396354
1954 Chestnut 1.62 m
Lic.: HANN

ADLERFLUT 🐴✓
HANN 276331315938752
Hauptstutbuch
1952 Chestnut

CODEX 🐴✓
HOLST 276321210384362
1962 Brown 1.59 m
Lic.: BWP, HOLST

LATOUCHA 🐴✓
BWP 056002W00011389
Stb.
1965 Brown

DER LOEWE XX 🐴✓
xx 1944

ALTWUNDER 🐴✓
HANN 1950

ABLEGER I 🐴✓
HANN 1942

DICHTERSPIEL 🐴✓
HANN 1944

COTTAGE SON XX 🐴✓
xx 1944

ETTAL 🐴✓
HOLST 1946

FAUST 🐴✓
Sgldt 1959

ATOUCHA 🐴✓
BWP 1959
1.30m Jump. Level 2 Test 2 / Medium

💧 29.10% 🐎 INBREEDING COEFFICIENT

Darco, a Belgian Warmblood stallion bred by M. Paesen, became a cornerstone of modern Belgian sport horse breeding. With a stellar showjumping career under Ludo Philippaerts and an unparalleled legacy as a sire, Darco cemented his reputation as one of the greatest stallions in equestrian history.

Pedigree and Early Promise

Darco hailed from a remarkable dam line that blended power and refinement. His dam, **Ocoucha**, was by the influential Codex, out of Latoucha xx, adding Thoroughbred elegance and stamina to his genetic makeup. This combination produced a stallion of exceptional quality, characterized by intelligence, carefulness, and a tenacious work ethic.

Ludo Philippaerts, who partnered with Darco from the age of five, recalled his first impressions of the young stallion:

> "Together with Darco, I began my international career. He is a horse to remain grateful to for the rest of my life. Darco had everything it takes to make a unique super crack, as a showjumper as well as a sire. Horses of this outstanding quality remain great exceptions in the breeding industry."

A Stellar Competitive Career

Darco and Ludo Philippaerts became a legendary pair on the international showjumping circuit. Their partnership brought early success, including:

- **1988**: Winning their first World Cup qualifier at Olympia.
- **1989**: Another Volvo Cup victory at s'Hertogenbosch.
- **1990**: Sixth place at the World Equestrian Games in Stockholm.

- **1992**: Seventh place at the Barcelona Olympic Games.

Ludo attributed much of his success to Darco's intelligence, power, and stamina, qualities derived from his high-bred ancestors. As Ludo reflected:

> "I think Darco is one of the best stallions in the world. If you look at what his offspring are doing, he is very special – a top jumper and a top breeder. He has been unbelievable for Belgian breeding. Darco was a really careful horse himself, and his progeny are very honest horses with excellent character and mentality."

Breeding Legacy

While Darco's competitive achievements were extraordinary, his influence as a sire revolutionized Belgian breeding and extended globally. He was one of the first stallions to excel both in sport and in passing on his exceptional qualities to his progeny.

- **Approved Stallions**: Darco sired 188 approved stallions, ensuring his bloodlines would dominate breeding programs worldwide.
- **Top-Level Competitors**: He produced 212 offspring that competed successfully at 1.60m level, an astonishing achievement that underscores his prepotency as a sire.
- **Character and Versatility**: Darco's offspring were known for their honesty, good mentality, and exceptional jumping ability, making them desirable mounts for riders at all levels.

Famous Offspring

Darco's progeny include some of the most accomplished horses in showjumping history, many of whom became influential sires and dams in their own right:

- **Sapphire**: A double Olympic gold medalist with McLain Ward, known for her bravery and scope.
- **Narcotique de Muze**: A prolific broodmare who produced multiple international showjumpers.
- **Ogano Sitte**: A renowned sire whose offspring carry forward Darco's legacy.
- **Erco van't Roosakker**: Known for exceptional athleticism and breeding influence.
- **Nonstop**: A successful competitor and sire.
- **Udarco van Overis**: Another top-level jumper and sire.
- **Bamako de Muze**: A highly sought-after sire with international success.
- **Parco**: A consistent performer at the top level.
- **Winningmood**: A standout competitor known for his elegance and scope.

Influence on Belgian Breeding

Darco's impact on Belgian Warmblood breeding was transformative. He became the foundation of the breed, elevating its reputation on the global stage. His progeny's success brought international attention to Belgian breeding programs, solidifying their place among the world's elite.

Legacy

Darco passed away in 2006, but his influence remains unrivaled. His ability to consistently produce honest, talented, and versatile horses made him a cornerstone of modern sport horse breeding. His legacy lives on through his countless descendants, who continue to excel at the highest levels of competition and perpetuate his legendary bloodlines.

Darco's story is not just one of individual greatness but of a stallion who forever changed the landscape of equestrian sport and breeding. His name will remain synonymous with excellence, intelligence, and power—a true giant in the world of horses.

CHAPTER 18

NABAB DE RÊVE

1990

NABAB DE REVE 🟢🔵🟢
Stallion 1990 Brown 1.74 m
BWP 056002W00139797
BWP_Ambassadeur, Stb.
Lic.: BWP, SBS, SF
1.60m Jump.
Rider(s)

FEI (BEL05740)

BREEDER: DE BRUYN STEPHAN

QUIDAM DE REVEL 🟢🔵🟢
SF 25000182604507R
Stb.
1982 Brown 1.68 m
Lic.: BWP, HANN, HOLST, KWPN, MIPAAF, SF, ...
1.60m Jump.

MELODIE EN FA 🔵🟢
SF 25000178141191X
1978 Chestnut

JALISCO B 🔵🟢
SF 25000175000588W
1975 Brown 1.74 m
Lic.: SF
1.60m Jump.

DIRKA 🔵🟢
SF 25000150253086E
Elite
1969 Dark brown
1.60m Jump.

ARTICHAUT 🔵🟢
SF 25000160003401L
1966 Chestnut 1.68 m
Lic.: SF

CARAVELLE 🔵🟢
SF 25000150066111N
1968 Chestnut

ALME 🔵🟢
SF 1966
1.60m Jump.

TANAGRA 🔵🟢
SF 1963

NANKIN 🔵🟢
SF 1957

ONDINE DE BAUGY 🔵🟢
SF 1958

PIERREVILLE 🔵🟢
SF 1959

JARIOSE 🔵🟢
SF 1953

BEL AVENIR 🔵🟢
SF 1945

UNIVERS 🔵🟢
SF 1964

💧 61.52% 🐎 INBREEDING COEFFICIENT

95

Nabab de Rêve, a son of Quidam de Revel, was bred by Stephan de Bruyn at Haras de Rêve in Belgium but registered in France. Known for his versatility, consistency, and the remarkable influence he has had on breeding, Nabab de Rêve became a cornerstone of modern showjumping. While his competitive career was marked by strong team performances rather than individual glory, his legacy as a sire has made him one of the most influential stallions in the sport.

Pedigree: A Lineage of Excellence

Nabab de Rêve's bloodlines are steeped in greatness. His sire, **Quidam de Revel**, is a legendary showjumping stallion and a household name in equestrian breeding. His dam, **Melodie en Fa**, was by **Artichaut**, a sire renowned for producing international-level jumpers, including Quartz du Vallon and Orchestre, the latter achieving great success with McLain Ward. Artichaut also sired Muguet de Manoir, who was a top sire in France for two consecutive seasons.

Nabab inherited the power, scope, and temperament of his remarkable lineage, traits he consistently passed on to his progeny.

Competitive Career

Under the guidance of Belgian rider Philippe Lejeune, Nabab de Rêve became a dependable team player on the international stage. While he did not claim numerous individual accolades, his contributions to Belgian showjumping teams were invaluable.

- **2001 Aachen Nations Cup**: Nabab de Rêve was instrumental in Belgium's victory, with only one rail in the second round.

- **2001 European Championships (Arnhem)**: Finished 45th individually, playing a solid supporting role.
- **2002 World Equestrian Games (Jerez)**: Helped Belgium secure the team bronze medal, finishing 42nd individually.

Lejeune praised Nabab de Rêve for his reliability, scope, and ability to perform consistently under pressure—a quality that translated seamlessly into his role as a sire.

Breeding Legacy

Nabab de Rêve's greatest achievements lie in the breeding shed. As a stallion, he became a prolific producer of top-level showjumpers and stallions. His influence on breeding is vast, with progeny competing on the world stage and dominating WBFSH rankings.

- **Approved Stallions**: Nabab sired **72 approved stallions**, perpetuating his legacy across generations.
- **Top-Level Competitors**: He produced **132 horses competing at 1.60m level**, a testament to his prepotency.

Notable Offspring

The list of Nabab de Rêve's progeny reads like a who's-who of modern showjumping. His sons and daughters are celebrated for their athleticism, temperament, and consistency in the ring.

1. **Vigo d'Arsouilles**:
   Nabab's most famous son, Vigo d'Arsouilles, was crowned **Belgian Horse of the Year (2008)** and achieved global stardom by becoming the **World Champion at the 2010 WEG in Lexington**. Vigo's blend of power, scope, and elegance set him apart as a true superstar and a sire in his own right.

2. **London**:
   Aptly named, London finished **second individually at the London Olympics** and later competed for Glock under Gerco Schröder, earning numerous accolades, including **third place in the 2014 Madrid Grand Prix**.
3. **Kashmir van Schuttershof**:
   A foundation sire, Kashmir van Schuttershof has had an immense influence on modern breeding, producing countless top competitors.
4. **Glasgow WH Merelsnet**:
   A standout jumper, Glasgow embodies the athleticism and scope of Nabab's lineage.
5. **Nimrod de Muze**:
   A rising star among Nabab's progeny, continuing his legacy in sport and breeding.
6. **Prince van de Wolfsakker**:
   Known for his exceptional jumping ability and competitive success.

Representation on the World Stage

Nabab de Rêve's impact extended to the Olympics, where his progeny represented the pinnacle of showjumping excellence:

- **London 2012**: Nabab was represented by three offspring—Vigo d'Arsouilles, London, and Valentina van 't Heike—while his son Kashmir van Schuttershof also had a competitor in the event.

Rankings and Recognition

Nabab de Rêve consistently ranked among the top sires in the WBFSH standings, further solidifying his legacy:

- **2012**: Ranked 8th, with standout performances from London and Exquis Walnut de Muze.
- **2013**: Ranked 14th, with London as his top point-earner.
- **2014**: Ranked 15th, a testament to his continued influence in breeding.

Legacy

Nabab de Rêve's story is one of consistency, reliability, and generational impact. While his competitive career highlighted his role as a team player, his legacy as a sire has forever changed the landscape of showjumping and breeding.

His progeny's success on the world stage and his enduring influence in breeding programs worldwide ensure that Nabab de Rêve's name will remain synonymous with excellence in equestrian sport for generations to come.

CHAPTER 19

CASSINI I
1988

Cassini I in 2011, Photo Janne Bugtrup

CASSINI I 🔵🟢
Stallion 1988 Grey 1.72 m
HOLST 276321210021688
Lic.: HOLST, RHEIN, SF
1.60m Jump.
Rider(s)

CAPITOL I 🔵🟢
HOLST 276321210615475
1975 Grey 1.69 m
Lic.: HOLST

CAPITANO 🔵🟢
HOLST 276321210398668
1968 Grey 1.62 m
Lic.: HESS, HOLST

CORPORAL 🔵🟢
HOLST 1963
1.40m Jump.

RETINA 🔵🟢
HOLST 1952
1.60m Jump.

FOLIA 🔵🟢
HOLST 276321210460603
Hauptstutbuch
1969 Brown 1.67 m

MAXIMUS 🔵🟢
HOLST 1963
1.50m Jump.

VASE 🔵🟢
HOLST 1961

WISMA 🔵🟢
HOLST 276321210059284
Hauptstutbuch
1984 Brown 1.73 m

CALETTO II 🔵🟢
HOLST 276321210093778
Siegerhengst
1978 Dark brown 1.69 m
Lic.: HOLST

COR DE LA BRYERE 🔵🟢
SF 1968

DEKA 🔵🟢
HOLST 1967

PRISMA 🔵🟢
HOLST 276321210036578
Hauptstutbuch
1978 Grey 1.68 m

MAHMUD 🔵🟢
HOLST 1967

CERENA 🔵🟢
HOLST 1966

💧 44.34% 🐎 INBREEDING COEFFICIENT

101

Cassini I (1988), a Holsteiner stallion bred by the Levallois family, is a name synonymous with greatness in showjumping. Ridden by Eric Levallois, Cassini I not only achieved remarkable success in the ring but also established himself as a cornerstone of modern sport horse breeding. Renowned for his impeccable pedigree, stunning athleticism, and unparalleled ability to pass on his qualities to his offspring, Cassini I remains one of the most influential stallions in equestrian history.

A Pedigree of Distinction

Cassini I was sired by **Capitol I**, one of the most successful and sought-after sires in Holsteiner history, known for producing horses with extraordinary jumping ability, power, and rideability. His dam, **Wisma**, was by Caletto II, another Holsteiner legend, whose bloodlines are revered for their refinement, scope, and movement.

This exceptional lineage made Cassini I the perfect embodiment of the Holsteiner breed's hallmark traits: athleticism, intelligence, and versatility.

Competitive Career

Under the skilled guidance of Eric Levallois, Cassini I excelled in international showjumping, competing at the highest levels and showcasing his exceptional talent:

- **Gold Medalist at the European Young Rider Championships**: Cassini I demonstrated his immense potential early in his career.
- **International Grand Prix Success**: He consistently delivered top performances on the global stage, earning recognition as one of the top showjumpers of his era.

Cassini I's combination of power, technique, and reliability made him a crowd favorite and a valuable team member for the French national team.

Breeding Success

While Cassini I's competition career was stellar, his impact as a sire far exceeded even his own accomplishments. His ability to pass on his exceptional traits—scope, power, athleticism, and temperament—set him apart as one of the most important sires in modern breeding.

- **306 Approved Stallions**: Cassini I produced an astonishing number of approved stallions, ensuring his bloodlines are represented across generations.
- **200 Horses Competing at 1.60m Level**: His progeny's success at the highest levels of showjumping is a testament to his genetic influence.

The Traits of a Legend

Cassini I consistently stamped his offspring with the qualities that made him a standout:

- **Powerful, Balanced Movement**: His progeny display excellent canter mechanics and balance, making them highly rideable for all levels of competition.
- **Scope and Strength**: Horses by Cassini I are renowned for their ability to clear fences effortlessly.
- **Exceptional Temperament**: Known for their trainability and willingness, his offspring are a pleasure to work with, from amateurs to professionals.

Notable Offspring

Cassini I's influence is perhaps best demonstrated through the achievements of his remarkable progeny. His sons and daughters have excelled at the top levels of international showjumping, leaving an indelible mark on the sport:

1. **Berlin (Caspar)**:
   A multiple team gold medalist, Berlin played a crucial role in the Dutch team's victories at the 2006 World Equestrian Games in Aachen and the 2007 European Championships in Mannheim.

2. **Cumano**:
   A true superstar, Cumano won the individual gold medal at the 2006 World Equestrian Games in Aachen under Jos Lansink, cementing his place in history.

3. **Carambole**:
   Known for his consistency and power, Carambole has been a staple in international Grand Prix competitions.

4. **Eurocommerce Monaco**:
   An accomplished competitor at the highest level, Monaco was a consistent performer on the world stage.

5. **Clarimo**:
   A leading sire in his own right, Clarimo has produced numerous top-level jumpers, ensuring Cassini I's legacy continues to thrive.

Influence on Modern Breeding

Cassini I's impact on the breeding world is unparalleled. He is regarded as a foundation sire for the Holsteiner breed, but his influence extends far beyond Germany. Breeders worldwide continue to seek his bloodlines for their ability to produce consistent winners at the top levels of the sport.

Legacy

Cassini I's story is one of extraordinary achievement, both in the showjumping arena and in the breeding shed. His contributions to the sport horse industry are unmatched, and his influence continues to shape the future of equestrian sport.

A true legend of the Holsteiner breed, Cassini I's name will forever be synonymous with excellence, power, and the timeless qualities that define the very best in showjumping.

CHAPTER 20

❧

DIAMANT DE SÉMILLY
1991

DIAMANT DE SEMILLY 🟡⚜️✅
Stallion 1991 Dark brown 1.73 m
SF 25000191446545F
Lic.: AWR, BWP, CHS, HOLST, MIPAAF, SF, ZAN
1.60m Jump.
Rider(s)

FEI (FRA06880)

LE TOT DE SEMILLY ⚜️✅
SF 25000177037073A
1977 Chestnut 1.68 m
Lic.: AWR, SF
1.60m Jump.

GRAND VENEUR ⚜️✅
SF 25000160008795Y
1972 Chestnut 1.68 m
Lic.: SF
1.25m Jump.

AMOUR DU BOIS ⚜️✅
SF 1966

TANAGRA G ⚜️✅
SF 1963

VENUE DU TOT ⚜️✅
SF 25000150065553U
1965 Chestnut

JURISTE ⚜️✅
SF 1953

RELIQUE ⚜️✅
SF 1961

VENISE DES CRESLES ⚜️✅
SF 25000187354224F
Label élevage: excellente, Label modèle &
allures: excellente
1987 Brown

ELF III ⚜️✅
SF 25000160005200F
1970 Brown 1.70 m
Lic.: SF

IBRAHIM ⚜️✅
SF 1952

OSYRIS ⚜️✅
SF 1958

MISS DES CRESLES ⚜️✅
SF 25000178143639L
Label modèle & allures: élite
1978 Brown

AMARPOUR XX ⚜️✅
xx 1966

URLURETTE ⚜️✅
SF 1964

💧 51.37% 🐎 INBREEDING COEFFICIENT

107

Born in 1991, **Diamant de Sémilly** is a Selle Français stallion who has set an unprecedented standard in the world of equestrian breeding. Recognized as **the number one showjumping sire in the world**, Diamant de Sémilly has maintained his position in the top three for over a decade. Since 2020, he has also become a prominent figure in eventing, entering the top 10 on the World Sires Rankings for this discipline. His ability to consistently transmit exceptional qualities to his offspring has earned him a legendary reputation as a stallion who is both easy to cross with mares and guaranteed to produce competitive, high-quality progeny.

Traits That Define Excellence

Diamant de Sémilly's progeny inherit a remarkable combination of physical and mental traits that make them stand out in both the showjumping and eventing arenas. These characteristics include:

- **Powerful Back and Excellent Balance**: Providing stability and precision over fences.
- **Extraordinary Scope and Strength**: Ensuring effortless jumps, even at the highest levels of competition.
- **Elegant Canter and Suppleness**: Allowing for smooth transitions and efficient turns on course.
- **Uncommon Willingness and Intelligence**: Making them highly trainable and reliable partners.

His offspring are not only top performers but are also sought-after in the market, known for their rideability and competitiveness at all levels.

A Star-Studded Competitive Career

Before rising to fame as a sire, Diamant de Sémilly enjoyed an illustrious international showjumping career. Trained and ridden by Eric Levallois, he demonstrated exceptional talent and consistency:

- **Fontainebleau Finals**: Diamant excelled in the 4-, 5-, and 6-year-old finals at Fontainebleau, signaling his potential as a future star.
- **Gold Medal at the 2002 World Equestrian Games (Jerez)**: A cornerstone of the French team, Diamant played a critical role in securing team gold.
- **Champion of France (2002)**: Highlighting his dominance at the national level.
- **Team Silver at the 2003 European Championships**: Another milestone in his glittering career.

Despite a promising start to the 2004 season, including victory at the **Grand Prix of Auvers**, a tendon injury forced Diamant to withdraw from the Athens Olympic Games. However, he returned to competition with triumphs in the **CSI*** Grand Prix of Saint-Lô and Caen in 2005 and the **Grand Prix of Liège** in 2006.

The Legacy of a Breeding Icon

While Diamant de Sémilly's competitive achievements are impressive, his true legacy lies in his unparalleled success as a sire. His genetic influence spans multiple continents, producing horses that excel across disciplines and are prized for their versatility, athleticism, and temperament.

- **306 Approved Stallions**: A testament to the consistent quality of his progeny.

- **200 Horses Competing at 1.60m Level**: Proof of his dominance in the upper echelons of international showjumping.

Progeny of Distinction

Diamant de Sémilly's offspring have earned their place among the best in the world, with many achieving remarkable success at the highest levels of competition. Some of his most famous progeny include:

1. **Quickly de Kreisker**: A Grand Prix superstar known for his power and consistency.
2. **Dominator 2000 Z**: A modern-day sensation, excelling in top-level showjumping.
3. **Mumbai**: A rising star in international competitions.
4. **Don VHP Z**: A stalwart competitor at 1.60m, known for his reliability and scope.
5. **Utamaro d'Ecaussines**: A Grand Prix regular and fan favorite.
6. **Like a Diamond van het Schaek**: Combining elegance and athleticism in the ring.
7. **Andiamo de Sémilly**: A versatile competitor and proven sire.
8. **Bond Jamesbond**: A standout jumper with exceptional power.
9. **Elvis Ter Putte**: A favorite among breeders for his outstanding genetics.
10. **Emerald van't Ruytershof**: A world-class jumper with an unforgettable style.
11. **Rock'n Roll Sémilly**: A testament to Diamant's ability to produce consistent winners.

Influence on Modern Breeding

Diamant de Sémilly's influence has extended far beyond his own lifetime. Breeders around the world seek his bloodlines to infuse their programs with his hallmark traits. He is celebrated not only for producing elite showjumpers but also for his ability to adapt to a wide variety of mares, making him a versatile and reliable choice for breeders.

A Timeless Legend

Diamant de Sémilly's name is synonymous with excellence, not just as a showjumper but as a sire whose influence continues to shape the future of equestrian sport. His enduring legacy is a reflection of his unparalleled ability to produce champions, making him a cornerstone of modern breeding and an eternal icon in the world of showjumping.

CHAPTER 21

QUIDAM DE REVEL
1982

QUIDAM DE REVEL 🟢♦️✔️
Stallion 1982 Brown 1.68 m
SF 25000182604507R
Stb.
Lic.: BWP, HANN, HOLST, KWPN, MIPAAF, SF, SW
1.60m Jump.
Rider(s)

FEI (FRA02446)

JALISCO B ♦️✔️
SF 25000175000588W
1975 Brown 1.74 m
Lic.: SF
1.60m Jump.

DIRKA ♦️✔️
SF 25000150253086E
Elite
1969 Dark brown
1.60m Jump.

ALME ♦️✔️
SF 25000160001122N
1966 Brown 1.66 m
Lic.: AWR, BWP, HANN, KWPN, SF
1.60m Jump.

TANAGRA ♦️✔️
SF 25000150015110Z
1963 Brown

NANKIN ♦️✔️
SF 25000160001408C
1957 Brown 1.64 m
Lic.: HANN, SF

ONDINE DE BAUGY ♦️✔️
SF 25000149017757D
1958 Chestnut 1.62 m

IBRAHIM ♦️✔️
SF 1952

GIRONDINE ♦️✔️
SF 1950

FURIOSO XX ♦️✔️
xx 1939

DELICIEUSE ♦️✔️
SF 1947

FRA DIAVOLO XX ♦️✔️
xx 1938

CONSTELLATION ♦️✔️
SF 1946

HARPHORTAS XX ♦️✔️
xx 1939

NADINE ♦️✔️
SF 1935

💧 64.45% 🐎 INBREEDING COEFFICIENT

Born in 1982, **Quidam de Revel** is one of the most iconic Selle Français stallions in the history of equestrian sport. Bred by Prince Amaury de Broglie and trained under the masterful hands of **Hervé Godignon**, Quidam de Revel carved a path of greatness as both a top competitor and a breeding phenomenon.

His influence is undeniable, both on the course and in the breeding shed. From his illustrious international career to his unmatched legacy as a sire, Quidam de Revel has set a benchmark for excellence that continues to resonate across the equestrian world.

A Competitive Career of Distinction

Under Hervé Godignon, Quidam de Revel dominated the showjumping scene, displaying unparalleled talent, power, and precision. Some of his career highlights include:

- **1990 Nations Cup and Grand Prix Wins**: Victories in New York and Dortmund, where the then eight-year-old stallion earned over one million Francs.
- **1991 European Championships**: Finishing fourth in the team event and sixth individually at La Baule.
- **Nations Cup Success in 1991**: Wins in Hickstead, second place in Rotterdam, and multiple top finishes, including seventh in Calgary and fifth at the World Cup Finals in Gothenburg.
- **1992 Barcelona Olympic Games**: Representing France, Quidam de Revel helped secure **team bronze** and achieved an impressive fourth-place finish individually.
- **Other Major Wins in 1992**: Victories in the Nations Cups of Rome and Dinard, as well as the Grand Prix of Rome.

After an illustrious career spanning over a decade, Quidam de Revel retired from competition in 2001 at the remarkable age of 19.

A Legacy in Breeding

Quidam de Revel's impact as a sire rivals—and perhaps surpasses—his achievements in the ring. His ability to transmit exceptional athleticism, intelligence, and scope to his offspring quickly became evident when his first foals were born in 1988. Over the years, he has been one of the most sought-after stallions in the world, producing generations of champions.

By the Numbers:

- **242 Approved Stallions**: Highlighting his dominance in the breeding world.
- **156 Offspring Competing at 1.60m+ Level**: A testament to his consistent production of top-tier talent.
- **Two Million-Euro Earners**: Descendants such as **Sterrehof's Calimero** (Marc Houtzager) and **Verdi TN** (Maikel van der Vleuten) have earned over €2 million in prize money each.

Quidam de Revel's bloodlines remain prevalent in the upper echelons of showjumping, with **10 offspring in the top 100 Hippomundo Stallion Rankings**, including **four in the top ten**. His enduring influence places him **fourth in the Hippomundo Stallion Rankings**, based on average prize money earned by his progeny.

Famous Progeny

Quidam de Revel's offspring have achieved remarkable success in both competition and breeding. Among his most renowned sons are:

1. **Verdi TN**: A cornerstone of Dutch showjumping, Verdi enjoyed a stellar career under Maikel van der Vleuten, earning over €2 million.
2. **Nabab de Rêve**: A team bronze medalist at the 2002 WEG under Philippe Le Jeune, Nabab has produced countless international competitors.
3. **Dollar de la Pierre (Tlaloc La Silla)**: Winner of team gold at the 2002 WEG with Reynald Angot.
4. **Sterrehof's Calimero**: A top international performer with numerous Grand Prix wins.
5. **Quel Homme de Hus**: A celebrated showjumper with consistent performances at the highest levels.
6. **Quaprice Bois Margot**: A highly influential sire with successful progeny.
7. **Guidam**: A KWPN-approved stallion with an exceptional record of producing elite offspring.
8. **Quite Easy I**: Known for producing versatile and rideable offspring.
9. **Rahotep de Toscane**: A leading figure in modern showjumping.
10. **Quasimodo Z**: Another major contributor to Quidam's lasting legacy.

Pedigree Power

Quidam de Revel's success as a sire can be traced to his **stellar pedigree**. He hails from the prestigious **Almé-Jalisco B bloodline**, a cornerstone of modern showjumping breeding.

- **Sire Line**: His sire, **Jalisco B**, was a prolific producer of champions, passing on athleticism, scope, and a winning temperament.
- **Dam Line**: His dam, **Dirka**, was an international winner under Nelson Pessoa and a ¾ sister to the legendary French stallion **Uriel**. This combination of top-tier genetics has ensured Quidam's unparalleled success as a progenitor of champions.

A Timeless Legacy

Even years after his passing, **Quidam de Revel** remains one of the most influential stallions in the world. His ability to produce offspring with exceptional athleticism, intelligence, and scope has solidified his status as a cornerstone of modern showjumping breeding.

Quidam de Revel's contributions to the sport extend beyond his competitive success. He has shaped the future of equestrian sport by producing a lineage of champions who continue to dominate the world stage. A true legend, his influence will endure for generations to come.

CHAPTER 22

KANNAN
1992

KANNAN GFE 🔵🔵🔵
Stallion 1992 Dark brown 1.72 m
KWPN 528003199204130
Stb.
Lic.: AES, AWR, BAVAR, BWP, HOLST, KWPN,
1.60m Jump.
Rider(s)

FEI (BEL05750)

BREEDER: STAL KRAMER, OUD-
BEIJERLAND (NED)

VOLTAIRE 🔵🔵🔵
HANN 276331310165679
pref, WFFS-free
1979 Brown 1.68 m
Lic.: BWP, HANN, KWPN, MIPAAF, OLDBG, ...
1.60m Jump.

CEMETA 🔵🔵
KWPN 528003198406392
keur, pref, prest
1984 Brown 1.63 m
1.30m Jump.

FURIOSO II 🔵🔵
SF 25000159040975B
1965 Chestnut 1.67 m
Lic.: BADWU, BAVAR, HANN, HESS, OLDBG...

GOGO MOEVE 🔵🔵
HANN 276331311332775
Hauptstutbuch
1975 Brown 1.63 m

NIMMERDOR 🔵🔵
KWPN 147STB-H
pref, Stb.
1972 Brown 1.68 m
Lic.: HOLST, KWPN, SF
1.60m Jump.

WOZIETA 🔵🔵
KWPN 528003198007422
pref, Stb.
1980 Brown 1.65 m

FURIOSO XX 🔵🔵
xx 1939

DAME DE RANVILLE 🔵🔵
SF 1947

GOTTHARD 🔵🔵
HANN 1949

MOSAIK 🔵🔵
HANN 1966

FARN 🔵🔵
HOLST 1959

RAMONAA 🔵🔵
NWP 1963

LE MEXICO 🔵🔵
SF 1970

ROZIETA 🔵🔵
KWPN 1975

💧 37.50% 🐴 INBREEDING COEFFICIENT

119

Born in 1992 and bred by Stal Kramer, **Kannan** is one of the most remarkable stories in modern equestrian history. Initially dismissed by the licensing commission, Kannan overcame early doubts to become a dominant force in international showjumping and breeding. His resilience, talent, and exceptional genetic legacy have cemented his place among the world's elite stallions.

Early Challenges and a Promising Start

Kannan's journey to stardom was anything but conventional. Rejected by the **KWPN licensing commission** during his initial inspection, Kannan did not receive KWPN status until 2011, when he was 19 years old. Despite this setback, his potential was evident under saddle, and he quickly gained recognition.

Purchased by **Guido Bruyninx**, Kannan began competing in the Belgian cycle for young jumpers, where he tied for first place. This early success led to his victory in the **six-year-old Belgian cycle**, earning him a spot at the **World Young Horse Championships in Lanaken**, where François Mathy Jr. guided him through the initial rounds.

It was during this period that Kannan caught the eye of the wife of French rider **Michel Hécart**, leading to his sale for a record price. This marked the beginning of a fruitful partnership between Kannan and Hécart, who found the stallion to be exceptionally trainable and eager to work.

Competitive Career

Under Michel Hécart, Kannan's natural abilities flourished. Hécart described him as a horse with excellent balance, a soft mouth, and a willingness to work. Recognizing the need for better physical conditioning, Hécart adjusted Kannan's routine to include extended time outdoors, improving his strength and fitness.

Kannan competed successfully at the international level, proving his value as both a competitor and a sire. His career was a testament to his adaptability, trainability, and resilience, qualities he passed on to his progeny.

In 2009, Kannan's career took another turn when he was sold to British stallion keeper **Kenneth Rehill**. However, his stay in England was brief. **Arnaud Evain**, head of the French Studbook Group GFE, recognized Kannan's extraordinary potential for breeding and brought him back to France. There, Kannan stood with spectacular success, solidifying his legacy as one of the most influential sires of the modern era.

A Legacy in Breeding

Kannan's contributions to breeding are extraordinary. Despite his initial rejection by the KWPN, his offspring have dominated the sport, consistently proving his ability to pass on exceptional traits, including athleticism, rideability, and a winning temperament.

By the Numbers:

- **190 Approved Stallions**: A testament to his influence on breeding programs worldwide.
- **190 Offspring Competing at 1.60m+ Level**: His progeny have excelled at the highest levels of international showjumping.

Famous Offspring

Kannan's legacy as a sire is perhaps his greatest achievement. His offspring have excelled in showjumping arenas around the globe, including Olympic and World Championship competitions. Some of his most notable progeny include:

1. **Quabri de L'Isle**: A superstar on the global stage, Quabri has been a consistent performer at the highest level of showjumping.
2. **Molly Malone V**: A mare renowned for her power and elegance, competing successfully with Bertram Allen.
3. **Nino des Buissonnets**: The 2012 Olympic individual gold medalist under Steve Guerdat, a shining example of Kannan's ability to produce champions.
4. **Toupie de la Roque**: A standout competitor on the international circuit.
5. **Dorai d'Aiguilly**: A top performer known for exceptional athleticism.
6. **Oh d'Eole**: A consistent competitor in Grand Prix classes worldwide.
7. **Paddock du Plessis**: Another exceptional athlete who exemplifies Kannan's influence in breeding.

Pedigree and Traits

Kannan's remarkable success as a sire can be attributed to his excellent pedigree and the traits he passes on with exceptional consistency. His offspring are known for their:

- **Balance and Rideability**: Making them ideal partners for riders at all levels.
- **Athleticism and Power**: Enabling them to excel in the most demanding competitions.
- **Trainable Temperament**: A hallmark of Kannan's progeny, ensuring their success in both sport and breeding.

A Timeless Influence

Kannan's journey from overlooked young stallion to one of the world's leading sires is a story of perseverance, talent, and extraordinary success. His influence continues to shape the sport of showjumping, with his bloodlines present in top horses worldwide.

Kannan's legacy is not just measured by his own achievements but by the incredible impact of his progeny. As a sire, he has redefined what it means to produce champions, leaving an indelible mark on the equestrian world.

CHAPTER 23

CLINTON
1993

CLINTON ✅🐴✅
Stallion 1993 Grey 1.70 m
HOLST 276321210236093
BWP_Ambassadeur
Lic.: BAVAR, BWP, HANN, HOLST, KWPN, MIPAAF, (
1.60m Jump.
Rider(s)

FEI (BEL06347)

BREEDER: GEORG CLAUSEN, RABENKIRCHEN
(GER)

CORRADO I ✅🐴✅
HOLST 276321210046185
1985 Grey 1.73 m
Lic.: HOLST, SF
1.60m Jump.

URTE 🐴✅
HOLST 276321210054982
1982 Brown 1.66 m
1.30m Jump.

COR DE LA BRYERE 🐴✅
SF 25000160011506B
1968 Dark brown 1.69 m
Lic.: HOLST, SF

SOLEIL 🐴✅
HOLST 276321210123680
Hauptstutbuch
1980 Grey 1.72 m

MASETTO 🐴✅
HOLST 276321210011776
1976 Grey
Lic.: HOLST

OHRA 🐴✅
HOLST 276321210010677
1977 Bay 1.67 m
1.50m jump.

RANTZAU XX 🐴✅
xx 1946

QUENOTTE 🐴✅
SF 1960

CAPITOL I 🐴✅
HOLST 1975

KUERETTE 🐴✅
HOLST 1973

MONTANUS 🐴✅
HOLST 1972

EMITA 🐴✅
HOLST 1968

LANDGRAF I 🐴✅
HOLST 1966

BRIKSCHA 🐴✅
HOLST 1965

🔺 48.44% 🐴 INBREEDING COEFFICIENT

Born in 1993 and bred by Georg Clausen of Rabenkirchen, **Clinton** is a stallion who epitomizes excellence in both the sport and breeding worlds. A striking grey Holsteiner, Clinton's legacy stems from his lineage, his stellar competition career, and the exceptional quality of his offspring. Combining two of Holstein's most influential bloodlines, Clinton has left an indelible mark on modern showjumping.

Pedigree and Physical Characteristics

Clinton's pedigree represents the best of Holsteiner breeding. He is the product of a cross between two legendary C lines:

- **Sire: Corrado I** – Known for his international success with Franke Sloothaak, Corrado I brought precision and power to Clinton's lineage.
- **Damline: Capitol I** – Renowned for producing powerful jumpers, Capitol I added immense scope and strength to Clinton's genetic makeup.

Physically, Clinton was a large-framed stallion with striking presence and a smooth topline. With heavy bone, correct legs, and substantial substance, he was built to excel. While his jumping technique lacked the bascule desired in today's showjumpers, his athleticism, movement, and boldness made him an exceptional competitor and a strong producer of quality offspring.

Clinton's breeding required careful pairing. To maximize his potential, he needed mares with high levels of Thoroughbred blood—an element not widely available during his prime breeding years.

A Strategic Start

Clinton's journey to the breeding spotlight was not without its challenges. Initially bred in Holstein, he was sold as a young stallion to Dutch breeder **Henk Nijhof**. Instead of presenting Clinton for licensing with the KWPN, Nijhof chose a different path. Following his successful strategy with Heartbreaker, Nijhof sent Clinton to **Hubert Hamerlinck** in Belgium, where the stallion was licensed with the **Belgian Warmblood Studbook (BWP)**.

As Nijhof explained to *Horse International*:

> "Clinton is a boisterous stallion, and if we had put him through the performance test here [in Holland], chances were that he'd have come home again pretty quickly. You had to think very carefully about how to get some stallions in the circuit. If we had tried the KWPN straight away, we might not have them as breeding sires now."

This calculated decision allowed Clinton to build a reputation both as a competitor and as a breeding stallion.

Competitive Career

Clinton's career on the international stage was nothing short of remarkable. Ridden by **Dirk Demeersman**, Clinton became a regular name in top-level competitions. At the **2004 Athens Olympic Games**, the pair achieved a fifth-place finish in the overall rankings, tackling massive courses with ease and precision.

Clinton's other notable achievements include:

- **2006**: Victory at Beervelde, 2nd in the Lumen Grand Prix, and 4th at Wiesbaden.

Clinton's boldness, power, and athleticism made him a formidable force in the ring.

A Legacy in Breeding

Thanks to the modern trend of combining sport and stud careers, Clinton was able to make an impact both in the arena and in the breeding barn. His success as a sire is undeniable, producing numerous offspring that have excelled on the international stage.

By the Numbers:

- **89 Approved Stallions**: A testament to his influence on breeding programs worldwide.
- **100 Offspring Competing at 1.60m+ Level**: Highlighting the exceptional quality of his progeny.

Famous Offspring:

Clinton's legacy is perhaps best exemplified through his most notable offspring:

1. **Cornet Obolensky**: Arguably Clinton's most famous son, Cornet Obolensky has become a legend in his own right, excelling in competition and as a sire.
2. **Eldorado van de Zeshoek TN**: A powerhouse in breeding, known for producing top-class jumpers.
3. **Suspens Floreval**: A consistent performer at the highest levels.
4. **Utrillo van de Heffinck**: An international competitor and sire of champions.
5. **Upsilon van de Heffinck**: Another standout jumper with a strong presence in breeding.

Clinton's ability to produce high-caliber offspring lies in his genetic legacy and his ability to transmit traits such as power, boldness, and athleticism.

A Lasting Impact

Clinton's story is one of determination, strategy, and undeniable talent. From his beginnings as a bold and boisterous young stallion to his success as a competitor and sire, Clinton has shaped the future of modern showjumping.

His influence continues to be felt through his offspring, many of whom have achieved incredible success in sport and breeding. Clinton's legacy serves as a reminder of the importance of strategic decisions in breeding and the enduring power of exceptional bloodlines.

Through his contributions to both the sport and the breeding world, Clinton has earned his place as one of the greats in equestrian history.

CHAPTER 24

❧

BERLIN
1994

BERLIN 🟢🔵🟢
Stallion 1994 Grey 1.74 m
HOLST 276321210274394
pref
Lic.: HANN, HOLST, KWPN, OLDBG, OS, RHEIN, SE
1.60m Jump.
Rider(s)

FEI (GER18692)

BREEDER: JOSEF UNKELBACH, KOLN (GER)

CASSINI I 🔵🟢
HOLST 276321210021688
1988 Grey 1.72 m
Lic.: HOLST, RHEIN, SF
1.60m Jump.

ESTIA 🔵🟢
HOLST 276321210025090
Hauptstutbuch
1990 Brown 1.72 m
1.60m Jump.

CAPITOL I 🔵🟢
HOLST 276321210615475
1975 Grey 1.69 m
Lic.: HOLST

WISMA 🔵🟢
HOLST 276321210059284
Hauptstutbuch
1984 Brown 1.73 m

CARETINO 🟢🔵🟢
HOLST 276321210242583
Stb.
1983 Brown 1.68 m
Lic.: HOLST, KWPN, MIPAAF, SF, SWB
1.60m Jump.

VARDANA 🔵🟢
RHEIN 276343434209183
Hauptstutbuch
1983 Brown 1.63 m

CAPITANO 🔵🟢
HOLST 1968

FOLIA 🔵🟢
HOLST 1969

CALETTO II 🔵🟢
HOLST 1978

PRISMA 🔵🟢
HOLST 1978

CALETTO II 🔵🟢
HOLST 1978

ISIDOR 🔵🟢
HOLST 1972

FERNANDO 🔵🟢
HOLST 1976

OSTIA 🔵🟢
HOLST 1977
1.60m Jump.

💧 41.21% 🐎 INBREEDING COEFFICIENT

Born in 1994 and bred by **Josef Unkelbach of Cologne**, **Berlin** is a Holsteiner stallion whose illustrious career as both a showjumper and a sire has cemented his place in equestrian history. Under the skillful guidance of Dutch rider **Gerco Schröder**, Berlin was a cornerstone of the Dutch showjumping team, contributing to gold medal victories on the world's biggest stages. With his impeccable jumping ability, exceptional temperament, and remarkable scope, Berlin's legacy thrives through his offspring.

Competitive Career: A Legacy of Gold

Berlin's journey to the top of the sport began early, with his natural talent catching the eye of esteemed riders and trainers. Initially trained by **Stefanie Fleer**, Berlin's potential as a young stallion stood out, and by the time he was six years old, he had drawn the attention of **Jan Tops**, who sold him to **Euro commerce**.

Berlin first entered the international spotlight under **Wim Schröder**, Gerco's older brother. Together, the pair achieved significant success, including:

- **2002**: Victory in the Grand Prix of Valkenswaard (1.50m).
- **2004**: Win at the Grand Prix of Verona.
- **2003 European Championships in Donaueschingen**: A 12th-place finish in Berlin's first senior championship appearance.

In 2005, Wim Schröder suffered an injury, and Berlin's reins were passed to Gerco Schröder. The change marked the beginning of Berlin's rise to legendary status.

Key Achievements with Gerco Schröder:

1. **2006 European Championships (Mannheim)**: Berlin was instrumental in securing team gold for the Netherlands.
2. **2006 World Equestrian Games (Aachen)**: The pinnacle of Berlin's career came at the WEG, where he delivered a decisive clear round to secure another team gold. Berlin finished sixth individually, a testament to his consistency and ability to compete at the highest level.
3. Victories in prestigious Grand Prix events, including **La Coruña, Valkenswaard**, and **Verona**.
4. **2006 Dutch National Champion**: Showcasing his dominance in domestic competition.

Gerco Schröder recalls Berlin's unforgettable performance at the WEG in Aachen:

> "I will never forget the last round at the World Equestrian Games in Aachen in 2006. He jumped fantastic and made sure we won gold with the team at the WEG! That's something you normally only dream about."

Traits and Temperament

Berlin's success in the ring was built on a combination of physical and mental attributes. Gerco highlighted the stallion's best qualities:

- **Scope**: Berlin possessed immense power and range, enabling him to tackle the most challenging courses with ease.
- **Disposition**: His calm and willing nature made him a joy to ride and train.

- **Carefulness**: A critical trait for a top showjumper, Berlin's careful jumping style allowed him to consistently deliver clear rounds.

These traits not only defined Berlin's career but also became hallmarks of his offspring.

Breeding Success

As a sire, Berlin has proven to be just as exceptional as he was in the arena. With **84 approved stallions** and **73 horses competing at the 1.60m level**, his impact on modern showjumping breeding is undeniable.

Famous Offspring:

1. **Caspar 232**: A top international performer, carrying on Berlin's legacy in the sport.
2. **Berlux Z**: A standout competitor with exceptional ability and scope.
3. **Bull Run's Faustino de Tili**: A successful showjumper known for his talent and consistency at the highest levels.

Berlin's offspring are known for their carefulness, good characters, and athleticism—qualities inherited from their illustrious sire.

A Lasting Legacy

Berlin's story is one of determination, talent, and success at every level of the sport. From his early days as a promising young stallion to his championship-winning performances under Gerco Schröder, Berlin's contributions to showjumping are unparalleled.

His achievements in both competition and breeding have ensured his place among the greats of Holsteiner history. As Gerco Schröder aptly puts it:

> "Berlin's scope and character are exceptional, and his legacy lives on through his offspring, who carry his qualities into the future of showjumping."

With gold medals, Grand Prix victories, and a lineage that continues to shape the sport, Berlin remains a shining example of the very best in equestrian excellence.

CHAPTER 25

∽

BALOUBET DU ROUET

1989

BALOUBET DU ROUET 🟢⊕⊘
Stallion 1989 Chestnut 1.70 m
SF 25000189502905H
Lic.: BWP, HANN, HOLST, SBS, SF, SWB
1.60m Jump.
Rider(s)

FEI (BEL05011)

BREEDER: M. LOUIS FARDIN (PERE),MME
LOUIS FARDIN, JUILLEY (FRA)

💧 45.90% 🐎 INBREEDING COEFFICIENT

GALOUBET A ⊕⊘
SF 25000160011039J
1972 Brown 1.73 m
Lic.: AWR, SF
1.60m Jump.

MESANGE DU ROUET ⊕⊘
SF 25000178141976T
1978 Chestnut
1.25m Jump.

ALME ⊕⊘
SF 25000160001122N
1966 Brown 1.66 m
Lic.: AWR, BWP, HANN, KWPN, SF
1.60m Jump.

VITI ⊕⊘
Trotter 25000150024304F
1965 Chestnut

STARTER ⊕⊘
SF 25000160002411M
1962 Chestnut 1.64 m
Lic.: SF

BADINE ⊕⊘
SF 25000150067279
1967 Chestnut

IBRAHIM ⊕⊘
SF 1952

GIRONDINE ⊕⊘
SF 1950

NYSTAG ⊕⊘
Trotter 1957

IDA DE BOURGOIN ⊕⊘
Trotter 1952

RANTZAU XX ⊕⊘
xx 1946

KAIRONNAISE ⊕⊘
SF 1954

BEL AVENIR ⊕⊘
SF 1945

PERLE DE NORVAL ⊕⊘
SF 1959

Baloubet du Rouet, a stallion born in 1989 and bred by M. Louis Fardin, stands as one of the most dominant and influential figures in the history of show jumping and horse breeding. His exceptional success on the competition circuit, combined with his unparalleled impact as a sire, has made him a true phenomenon in the equestrian world.

Unbeatable in Sport: A Partnership for the Ages

Together with his rider Rodrigo Pessoa, Baloubet du Rouet formed one of the most iconic combinations in show jumping history. During his peak years, Baloubet was virtually unstoppable. His performances were nothing short of extraordinary, resulting in an individual Olympic gold medal at the 2004 Athens Games and an unprecedented three consecutive FEI World Cup Final victories.

What set Baloubet apart was his incredible scope, reflexes, and boundless energy. He had a natural talent for jumping, consistently overcoming the toughest courses with ease. In addition to his technical prowess, Baloubet was also known for his mental fortitude—he thrived under pressure, always delivering when it mattered most. His combination of athleticism and temperament made him a horse ahead of his time, and he was ranked No. 1 in the world for several years.

Baloubet's achievements in the sport were not limited to individual accolades. His victories contributed significantly to the success of the Brazilian team, marking him as one of the greatest horses in modern show jumping. His partnership with Pessoa cemented their place in the history of the sport, with their combined victories resonating across international competitions.

The Legacy Continues: A Sire for the Ages

While Baloubet du Rouet's success in the ring is well-documented, his influence as a sire has proven to be equally remarkable. Ten years after retiring from competition, Baloubet once again made headlines, this time as a leader in the world of show jumping breeding. He has become a pillar of modern equine genetics, passing on his exceptional qualities to the next generation.

As a sire, Baloubet has produced horses that have achieved great success at the highest levels of the sport, with offspring competing at 1.60m—the pinnacle of show jumping. His progeny are known for inheriting his scope, reflexes, and careful jumping style, making them highly sought after in the competitive world.

Among his most famous offspring are:

- **Chaman** (ridden by Ludger Beerbaum)
- **Bubalu VDL** (Jur Vrieling)
- **Palloubet d'Halong** (Jessica Sprunger)
- **Sydney Une Prince** (Roger Yves Bost)

These horses, along with many others, have continued Baloubet's legacy, excelling in major international competitions and solidifying their place among the sport's top performers.

Baloubet du Rouet's impact extends beyond just producing top-level competitors. He has also proven to be an exceptional producer of broodmares, further expanding his influence in the breeding world. Notably, the stallion is the sire of the dam of **Explosion W**, the top show jumper ridden by Ben Maher, exemplifying his ability to produce progeny that excel both on the competition circuit and in breeding.

A Monumental Legacy in Breeding

Baloubet du Rouet's contributions to horse breeding are undeniable. To date, he has sired 116 approved stallions and 120 horses competing at the 1.60m level. His offspring continue to dominate the global show jumping scene, proving that his genetic influence is as potent as ever.

Among the many horses carrying Baloubet's name are:

- **Balou du Rouet** (one of his most successful sons, continuing his sire line)
- **Chaman**
- **Bubalu VDL**
- **Dubai du Cèdre**
- **Napoli du Ry**
- **Palloubet d'Halong**
- **Taloubet Z**
- **Sydney Une Prince**
- **Untouchable**
- **Falko de Hus**

These champions represent the pinnacle of Baloubet du Rouet's breeding achievements, each carrying forward his traits of scope, carefulness, and competitive drive.

A Legacy That Endures

Baloubet du Rouet's legacy is one of unparalleled success, both in sport and in breeding. From his gold medal in Athens to his record-breaking World Cup victories, he has left an indelible mark on the history of show jumping. As a sire, his influence continues to shape the future of the sport, producing horses that carry his exceptional qualities and compete at the highest levels.

His impact is not just measured by his own achievements, but by the continued success of his offspring, who carry on his genetic legacy. Baloubet du Rouet is not only a phenomenon in horse breeding—he is a living legend, whose influence will be felt for generations to come.

PART III

THE STALLIONS AND THEIR RIDERS

Legends in Show Jumping

CHAPTER 26

❧

GALOUBET A
&
GILLES-BERTRAN
DE BALANDA

The story of **Galoubet A** began when Jean-François Pellegrin, a prominent horseman, asked **Gilles Bertran de Balanda** to find a young stallion to develop. Gilles accepted the challenge and began attending young horse shows across France. It was at a competition in **Compiègne**, France, that a young stallion caught his attention. As they watched him warm up, **Marcel Rozier**, standing next to Gilles, shared his thoughts: while the horse wasn't the most academic in his jumping technique, there was something special about him. That horse was **Galoubet A**.

They started their journey together when Galoubet was five years old. Gilles didn't expect to qualify for the **French Championship** that same year, but under pressure from the owner, Jean-François Pellegrin, they achieved the impossible. After just three competitions, they qualified for the **Fontainebleau finals** and won the championship.

The partnership only grew stronger. At just seven years old, **Galoubet** and **Gilles** competed in the **European Championship** in **Rotterdam**, claiming victory. That same year, they also won the **French Senior Championship**, the **Aachen Nations Cup**, and the **World Equestrian Games** in **Dublin** in 1982. Galoubet continued to impress, finishing fifth at the **Olympic Games** in **Moscow**, solidifying their place in history.

While **Galoubet** never possessed the most refined jumping technique and lacked the ideal parabola over jumps, his willingness, bravery, and immense power were unmatched. Gilles often remarked that **Galoubet** never stopped, even as a young horse. Despite his sensitive nature and occasional distractions, when he was focused, he was a phenomenon in the ring. His incredible power and scope were unique—no other horse, before or after, matched his combination of heart and athleticism.

A memorable moment came during the **World Equestrian Games in Dublin** in 1982. In the first round, **Galoubet** was exceptional, and in the second, the French team needed a clear round to win the gold. **Gilles and Galoubet**, the last pair to go, rose to the pressure and delivered a clear round. They led the individual competition, with room for two rails down to secure the win. But as the final approached, the distraction of the closing ceremony—complete with carriages, ponies, and military bands—caused **Galoubet** to lose focus just before entering the ring. Despite Gilles' best efforts, the horse knocked down the first two jumps, and the dream of individual victory slipped away.

Nonetheless, **Galoubet A** and **Gilles-Bertran de Balanda** secured the **1982 Team Gold Medal** at the **World Equestrian Games** in Dublin, a testament to their bond and shared success.

CHAPTER 27

NARCOS II & ERIC NAVET

Eric Navet first took the reins of **Narcos II** after **Denis Brohier** started the stallion's training as a young horse. The duo went on to win numerous **Nations Cups** for the **French Team**. Narcos II was pre-selected for the **Seoul Olympics** as a reserve, though Philippe Rozier was ultimately chosen. Eric highlights Narcos' incredible bravery and mentality. Despite the less technical nature of courses at the time, Narcos' strength and courage made him a reliable partner.

Eric emphasizes the mentality and the braveness of Narcos.

"At that time the course was not as technical as nowadays but very impressive, composed of massive jumps: Narcos always gave me the confidence due to his power and braveness, that he will always jump the jumps, no matter the height. Narcos gave me real confidence in my riding".

The flaw of the stallion, if you have to find one, would be his slowness.

Narcos' pedigree is worth noting, particularly his dam, **Gemini** (by Tanael), produced four 1.60m level horses, including **Larry**, **Mazarin**, **Narcos II**, and **Quat'sous**. This exceptional breeding lineage stands out as a rare occurrence in the history of show jumping.

The influence of **Gemini** can also be seen in the French breeding program. In the 1980s, the **French studbook of Saint Lo** imported thoroughbred stallions to enhance their breeding lines, leading to the production of numerous exceptional horses, including Narcos II.

CHAPTER 28

QUITO DE BAUSSY & ERIC NAVET

Quito de Baussy, bred by **Eric Navet's** father, was truly a family horse. His pedigree, intertwined with the Navet family's history, is a testament to their deep-rooted connection to the sport. His dam, **Urgande B**, was a brave mare, whose history dates back to **World War II** when she narrowly escaped confiscation by the Germans. Eric's father had to present her to a German commission, but left her at the end of the line, thinking she would be taken. However, to his surprise, when he returned later that night, she was still there.

This remarkable mare produced Quito's mother, **Urgande B**, who played a pivotal role in his upbringing. Eric recalls that **Quito** showed exceptional ability from an early age. His balanced canter and smart jumping technique made him stand out. While not the most spectacular jumper, Quito was always correct and willing, regardless of the circumstances.

In 1990, at just eight years old, **Quito de Baussy** won the **World Cup Final in Bercy**, a record that still stands, as the FEI later restricted the competition to horses aged nine and older. **Quito** went on to win a remarkable six medals in five years, including:

- **1990**: Team and Individual Gold at the **World Equestrian Games** in **Stockholm**
- **1991**: Individual Gold at the **European Championship** in **La Baule**
- **1992**: Team Bronze at the **Barcelona Olympics**
- **1993**: Team Bronze at the **European Championship** in **Gijón**
- **1994**: Team Silver at the **World Equestrian Games** in **The Hague**

Despite his remarkable achievements, **Quito** was never fully recognized for his contributions to the sport, but his impact was undeniable. Throughout his career, he earned more than **4.5**

million Francs, solidifying his place as one of the most prolific stallions in the sport.

CHAPTER 29

∽

DIAMANT DE SEMILLY
&
ERIC LEVALLOIS

Arriving at **de Semilly Stud** in **February 1994, Diamant de Semilly** immediately impressed **Eric Levallois** with his natural ability. Despite being just four years old, he exhibited a level of intelligence and ease over jumps that was rare. Recognizing his potential, Eric decided to fast-track his training and take him straight to competition. By the end of his four-year-old season, Diamant was already excelling at the highest levels.

At the **2002 World Equestrian Games** in **Jerez de la Frontera**, the French team was aiming for gold, though they weren't entirely confident. Sadly, just a month before the Olympics, **Diamant de Semilly** suffered an injury, preventing him from participating. However, he was soon in demand for breeding, and Eric found it challenging to balance his competitive career with his role as a sire.

Sadly, Diamant de Semilly's career was cut short due to recurring colic and several surgeries. Despite this, his legacy lives on through his offspring, who are known for their intelligence, bravery, and heart. Eric fondly recalls his time with Diamant, particularly their performances in the **Aachen** and **Rome Nations Cups**. Diamant de Semilly gave his all in the ring, and Eric considers him the greatest pride of his career.

CHAPTER 30

_✧_

DARCO
&
LUDO
PHILIPPAERTS

Darco was a horse who made an indelible mark on **Ludo Philippaerts'** career. At just 5 years old, Ludo immediately recognized the horse's potential after jumping just three fences. Darco's incredible bloodlines and careful, powerful jumping style made him an invaluable partner. Despite his sometimes-challenging canter, Darco's willingness and determination made him a standout competitor.

In **1992**, **Darco** was injured just before the **Barcelona Olympics**, but after undergoing surgery, he returned to the top of his game. His career highlights include:

- **1990**: 6th at the **World Championships** in **Stockholm**
- **1992**: 7th at the **Barcelona Olympics**
- **1992**: Winner of the **Volvo World Cup** in **London**
- **Calgary**: 2nd in the richest Grand Prix in the world

Darco's legacy continues to live on, particularly through his offspring, many of whom have excelled at the highest levels of the sport, further cementing his place in the pantheon of show jumping legends.

ABOUT THE AUTHOR

MATHILDE CHEREAU

As a young girl, my father—who had a deep love for horses—shared his enthusiasm with me. I was instantly captivated by their physicality, grace, and the unique bond they share with humans. To this day, I strive to embody the horse's qualities of empathy and resilience in my own life.

I began my journey in the equestrian world in the classic "French" way: joining a pony club. At 15 years old, I had the incredible opportunity to participate in the Pony Eventing French Championship in 1990, held in Le Touquet, Normandy. It was an unforgettable experience that solidified my passion for the sport.

However, after my childhood experience with horses, life took me in a different direction. I moved to the United States to pursue my studies, and for nearly 20 years, I was distanced from the equestrian world. Despite this, I continued to follow high-level equestrian sport through the media.

Eighteen years ago, personal circumstances brought me back into the horse world. I began organizing national and international events in the south of France, and later, I built our own stables there. This led me to travel frequently to Belgium and Holland as a horse dealer, where I started to forge incredible connections within the high-level equestrian community.

The turning point came when I decided to begin breeding horses after my once-in-a-lifetime mare sustained an injury. She was only 6 years old, but I began breeding her purely for the joy it brought me. The experience was profoundly fulfilling, and it sparked my interest in the breeding world.

I was fortunate enough to further my breeding knowledge through an amazing partnership with VDL Stud and Marc Van Dijck, from whom I learned invaluable lessons.

Eventually, we decided to invest in a farm in Ocala, Florida, with the support of my family. Living in the U.S. while bringing European expertise with me, I saw significant opportunities to elevate the breeding knowledge here.

With the help of my friend, Mike Beas, I embarked on the journey of publishing this book. My goal is to introduce breeding stallions, offering valuable information to the public.

Writing this first volume made me realize just how passionate the equestrian community in Europe is about breeding. I hope this work sparks curiosity and deepens the understanding of breeding in the American equestrian world.

It's truly a remarkable passion, one that I am honored to share.

Follow:
Instagram // @MDStables
Facebook //@Mathilde Chereau

ABOUT THE AUTHOR

MICHAEL BEAS

Horses have always held a special place in my heart. I vividly remember my father, Frank Beas, taking me every weekend to see them in Florida, where I was born. He had a lifelong dream of owning a horse and watching it compete, but time never allowed him to fulfill that aspiration. I feel truly blessed to live out that dream for him, carrying forward his passion for horses through breeding at Beas Family Farms.

The journey of breeding horses has been both challenging and rewarding. Every step has been a learning experience—whether from more seasoned riders, breeders, or simply from those who share a deep love for these magnificent animals. Each day brings new lessons and a deeper appreciation for the art of horse breeding.

At Atlas Elite Publishing, we've spent nearly a decade publishing and marketing books, with over a thousand titles brought to life under our Atlas imprint and through collaborations with our white-label partners. Just as the written word has the power to connect, inspire, and transform lives, the joy of nurturing and bringing sport horses into the world reminds me of the shared bonds we all hold as humans on this Earth.

I owe eternal gratitude to my wife, Kristine Kennedy Beas, for her unwavering support of my dreams—whether in writing, publishing, or horse breeding—and to my dear friend, Mathilde Chereau, for giving me the opportunity to join her on this incredible journey. Together, we continue to celebrate the beauty and passion of both storytelling and the equestrian world.

Visit:

www.atlaselitepublishing.com

Follow:

Instagram: @BeasMichael

Instagram: @BeasFamilyFarms

Thank You & Appreciation

We would like to thank **Gilles Bertran de Balanda**, **James Gentleman** and **Ilana Halpern**, supporting us and giving us their time and precious thoughts in order to accomplish this incredible journey.

Useful Links for Researching Horses, Riders and Breeding

Research and Data

HorseTelex
https://www.horsetelex.com

Hippomundo
https://www.hippomundo.com

Rimondo
https://www.rimondo.com

USEF
https://www.usef.org

Fédération Equestre Internationale
https://www.fei.org